Teach Me Mommy

Teach Me Mommy

A Preschool Learning Guide

First Revised Edition

by Jill Dunford
Illustrated by Tim Armstrong

Writer's Digest Books

Cincinnati, Ohio

First revised edition, 1985

Library of Congress Cataloging in Publication Data

Dunford, Jill.
  Teach me mommy.

  Includes bibliographies.
  Includes index.
  1. Education, Preschool—Curricula—Handbooks, manuals, etc. 2. Creative activities and seat work—Handbooks, manuals, etc. 3. Play groups—Handbooks, manuals, etc. 4. Domestic education—Handbooks, manuals, etc. 5. Children's literature—Bibliography. I. Title.
LB1140.4.D85 1985   649'.51   85-11926
ISBN 0-89879-187-1 (previously published by Gloucester Crescent, ISBN 0-931151-152-7)

To Matthew, Heather, Clayton, Adam, Benjamin, Bryan, and Brittany—
without whom none of this would ever have come about!

ACKNOWLEDGMENTS

It has been nearly four years since my magazine article about our home nursery school was published. There have been so many friends and acquaintances who have faithfully encouraged me to put our program down on paper for others. Thanks should go to Kathy Baer for her many phone calls and letters urging me to keep at this book. Also, a special thanks to Kathie Larsen for her creative ideas. A terrific mother, she really helped me gel the concept of the whole book.

Of course, the delightful illustrations would not have been possible without the talents of Tim Armstrong. His expertise came along at just the right time, when things did not seem as though they would ever come together.

My parents, Clarence and Nancy Wonnacott, have my sincere gratitude for always encouraging me to do my best and to go beyond myself. The extra time that they spent teaching and reading to me has carried over to my raising of my own children.

Most of all, my deep gratefulness goes to my husband, Robert, for having the faith in me and for helping me to get my ideas from file folders to book form. He has been my strongest support and strength.

CONTENTS

INTRODUCTION

WHY HAVE A HOME NURSERY SCHOOL?

Ten years ago, when our oldest son, Matthew, was four, I, perhaps like you, explored the various nursery schools to which we might send him. The choice was based on their reputation, cost and the distance from our home. The choices narrowed to two.

The first was a co-op group, which was inexpensive, but that required the mothers to help a certain amount of time each month. With two other preschoolers, I would have had to find a baby-sitter for them on those days, an impossibility at the time, from both a cost and time standpoint.

The second school required no time on my part, and though quite expensive, seemed the best choice.

After several weeks, however, I found my son becoming more and more unhappy. He enjoyed school, but would return home tense and demanding. He acquired some new words I didn't like. I felt that something was going wrong somewhere.

So my husband and I sat down to analyze exactly what our purpose was in sending Matthew to preschool. We knew we wanted him to gain social skills and become familiar with a school learning structure before he started kindergarten. We also wanted to help him broaden his horizons and get to know the world in which he lived.

As we talked about what we wanted for him, an idea began to form—why couldn't we have our own nursery school just for our children? The more we thought about it, the better the idea sounded.

We talked with several preschool experts in both the public school system and private schools. One of these experts said she personally would like to see all families do what we were considering doing. She felt that the nurturing time between a mother and child was much more important at this age than the associations he could be making with other children.

With this kind of encouragement, I read a lot of books and periodicals and studied the curriculum used in the child development preschool at a nearby state university. I talked to teachers and visited a number of preschools. Then, on a trial-and-error basis, I developed our program.

My four year old can't wait for nursery school time with me. I try to time it so my baby is down for a nap. When I have had younger children "attending" too, their attention span has naturally not been as long, so I provided them with toys to amuse themselves. Three seems to be the best age to actually begin this program with your child.

Nursery school has been a good opportunity for my older children to help prepare things for the little ones to use. They help mount pictures and clip stories. Many times, one in kindergarten has mentioned a story he has just read or something he has done in school that I can use. On days when they have been out of school because of snow, the older children have even been the teachers.

As I consider the program, now in its tenth year, I have reached several conclusions. It is a wonderful opportunity for me to spend quality, nurturing time with my children. Even when the baby is awake and the two year old is restless, the ratio of teacher to children is still only one to three, which is much better than in any commercial nursery program. I don't know a child who wouldn't rather spend time with his own mother playing, reading and learning.

Our children have no problems adjusting to school. Because they have adjusted to learning situations in our home, they are eager and willing to start kindergarten.

I also have been able to control the material being taught to my children. My purpose in having a home nursery is not to try to teach our children to read or count at an early age, but to look to us, their parents, as sources of knowledge and understanding. I don't pressure them to develop more quickly than they are ready, though I do teach skills such as the handling of scissors, crayons, glue and books. But primarily I try to help them have confidence in their ability to learn and to understand what others will be teaching them in the future.

There is a definite amount of time involved in preparation and organization for each day's study. But this manual will make it easier for you. We all spend time each week doing housework, cooking meals, etc. Isn't time spent for our children well worth it? After the initial preparation and material gathering, the work is minimal.

The most important thing is that you be with them! The time that a mother has with her child before he starts school passes so quickly. It is so important that children have the loving attention of their parents as much as possible.

Once, after one of our children visited an excellent nursery school, he came home saying that he liked our nursery school better because he could be with Mommy. I knew then that all the effort was worth it. There are few joys equal to teaching your children within the walls of your own home!

CHAPTER 1
GETTING STARTED

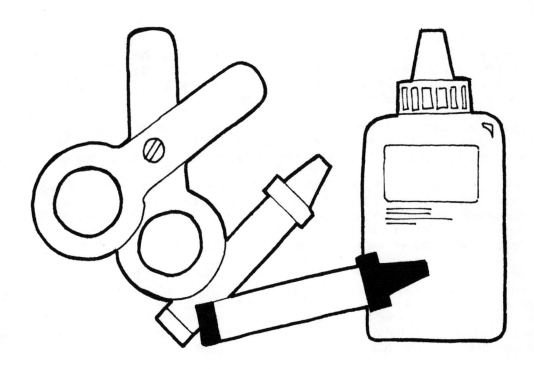

GETTING STARTED

This book contains the directions you will need to begin and develop your home nursery school. The steps are simple, and little equipment is needed. The materials are geared to children from ages three to five, although many of the ideas can be used for older children as well.

First, make a file folder or large manila envelope for each subject that you will be covering during the year. (See Table of Contents for suggested subjects.) Then, begin to fill them with ideas you find. My husband and I went through old magazines and catalogs to find pictures I could use. The public library is a rich resource for books on various subjects, including craft ideas that can be incorporated into various themes.

As I have continued through the years, I have found new pictures and stories to add. I even looked through recipe books to find treats and surprises that could be used with some of the topics. As you go along, you'll find many new ideas and sources that you will want to add.

Next, develop a simple plan for each day. Our school is set up for three days a week, for one and a half to two hours a day. If that is too much for you, begin with twice a week. The important thing is that, barring emergencies, once you have set the time, stick with it! Schedule appointments or other activities for nonschool days or times. Your children will quickly learn when you will be meeting and will need that order in their lives.

The weekly outline I use is included at the end of this chapter. It is based on the format used in the various chapters of this book. By filling out the outline in advance, you can quickly see the things you will need that week and what you need to plan for. *Remember to gear your activities to the skills of your children.* Three year olds will become frustrated if they are expected to be proficient with scissors, but a five year old can easily master that skill. Don't pressure them to do things they are not ready for yet.

Now let's discuss the steps used in these chapters.

INTRODUCTION: Begin each day with some introduction time. This is when you acquaint your children with the day's material. Most of what you need to say is written out for you, but you will want to add your own thoughts. We spend from five minutes to half an hour at this time, depending on the material and the attention span of the child. The introductions have deliberately been kept simple. If your child wants to know more, that's when you turn to an encyclopedia or other books to help them increase their knowledge and answer their questions.

BOOKS: Next, we read one or more books that will reinforce what we have learned in the introduction. I have included many that we have liked and reread through the years. I try to find these books at the library several weeks in advance, so that I can make adjustments and changes in the lessons if I need to. You will want to add to this bibliography as you find other books that your children enjoy. We have also purchased many of our favorites, which are now well loved and well worn!

MUSIC: Many chapters have little fingerplays and songs that the children can act out. There are a number of fun songbooks for children that you might want to use. Here are several that I like:

Musical Games, Fingerplays and Rhythmic Activities for Early Childhood, Marian Wirth

Children's Favorites, A Walt Disney Story Tape with 25 familiar songs and words in a book and tape.

Piggyback Songs and **More Piggyback Songs,** new songs sung to the tunes of childhood favorites, from Totline Press. (These are full of songs for all subjects.)

Children love music and sometimes need only a record or song to get them walking like elephants or flying like airplanes. Feel free to get into the act and don't be inhibited. Children love it when their mothers act and play with them.

CRAFTS AND ACTIVITIES: Next comes activity time. I have provided several crafts or activities to choose from for each day. Some require a lot of preparation, and others involve a short drive in your car. Choose what works best for your child or children and for your time. *Remember, you don't have to do all the crafts listed—you may pick just one.* That saves new ones for the next year, too.

TREATS: In many lessons, I have suggested appropriate treats for what you are studying. You may also want to save these treats for the preschooler to share with Daddy and the whole family at dinner time. You can make appropriate substitutions if salt or sugar intake is a problem. I have found that at least a glass of juice and a cracker is a nice way to end our time together.

EQUIPMENT

Here are some items that I use a lot. Make sure you have them in advance, so you aren't hunting for a pair of scissors while your child is waiting impatiently. An empty orange crate will hold just about everything listed here except the newsprint paper.

1. Crayons: a box of 16 or 24 is enough for a four year old. The big fat ones are nice for younger children. An elementary art teacher once told me to take off all the paper on the crayons so that the children can use both the small tips and the long sides to color—it's true!

2. Markers: these should mainly be used by you to draw the outlines of pictures that the children will then color. Choose washable ones in case of accidents!

3. Construction paper: large multicolored pads will be invaluable.

4. Butcher or newsprint paper: available from school supply stores—or many newspapers will let you have the ends of rolls for free. This is good where large sheets of paper are needed to draw the children's outlines or to cover cardboard boxes.

5. Cardboard: my husband saves the backs of pads of paper from work to back stand-up animals, pictures, etc.

6. Tempera: powdered paint available from a craft, art supply or school supply store; I mix some up in small baby food jars and use for everything. It's nice because it's washable.

7. Glue: a quick-drying "craft glue" is best. It is available at most craft or hobby stores. It is thicker than ordinary white glue and dries more quickly.

8. Glue stick: easy for younger children to handle when gluing.

9. Spray adhesive: nice for gluing large sheets of paper to cardboard or construction paper; use in garage or outside, only by you!

10. Scissors: your child should learn to use a good, blunt pair of scissors by the time he is four.

11. Glitter and sequins: these are optional—messy, but fun from time to time.

12. Catalogs or magazines: save some of these as picture resources for families, clothing, homes, etc.

13. Pipe cleaners: these come in handy for insect antennas, Christmas decorations, animals, etc. I prefer the white ones which can be colored with a marker or paint, but the colored ones are fine, too.

14. Dried beans, peas, macaroni, etc.: good for collages, fish and turkey pictures, etc.

15. Wiggly eyes: these plastic eyes come in various sizes and are available at craft or hobby shops. They're fun to use sometimes instead of traditional paper cutout eyes.

16. Ink pad: used for fingerprint animals, vegetable printing.

17. Stickers: available from gift shops, craft or hobby stores, stationery and school supply stores; good for making theme booklets, decorations for holidays, etc. With the great interest in stickers among kids today, you can find just about anything on a sticker!

RESOURCE MATERIAL

LIBRARY: You will probably get tired of hearing me talk about how wonderful the library is for your nursery planning, but it's true. I go about every three weeks, so that I'll have the books I'll need. The librarians are always willing to help you find things. Many libraries also have pictures of many subjects that you can check out, as well as records, filmstrips and movies that are appropriate if you have the equipment.

COMMUNITY: So many people are willing to take the time to share their talents with our children. A friend who is a police officer willingly showed his patrol car, even demonstrating the siren and lights. The firemen did a lot of extra things for the children, when I just had two of them for a tour. We traveled to a nearby farm, where the farmer's wife showed the children her chicken coop, the geese, and a cow with her new calf. She even showed the boys how she made butter out of cream! We chose a quiet time of the day for our bus ride, and the driver showed the children what levers he pushed to make the doors open and close and the token machine work. A friend who keeps bees invited the children over to watch out the window while he cleaned the honey out of the hives.

MAGAZINES: Here are several magazines, which consistently have good material for this age:

Ranger Rick's Nature Magazine—Older children—$10.50/yr.
Your Big Backyard—preschoolers—$8.50/yr.
National Wildlife Federation
1412 16th St. NW
Washington, DC 20036

These magazines have beautiful nature photographs, plus stories and activities. The children love looking at them.

The Friend—ages 3-12—$7.00/yr.
50 E. North Temple St.
Salt Lake City, UT 84150

This is a publication of the Latter Day Saints Church. It has good stories for preschoolers, plus many activities and easy recipes for kids.

Sesame Street Magazine—preschoolers—$9.95/yr.
P.O. Box 2895
Boulder, CO 80321

A colorful magazine for preschoolers using learning concepts and familiar friends from Sesame Street.

Turtle Magazine for Preschool Kids—$11.95/yr.
1100 Waterway Blvd.
Box 567
Indianapolis, IN 46206

This magazine emphasizes health, safety, exercise and good nutrition for preschoolers.

Highlights for Children—ages 2-12—$17.95/yr.
803 Church St.
Homesdale, PA 18431

This magazine has stories, activities, fingerplays, and historic and scientific articles for older children as well as preschoolers.

Most libraries carry one or more of these magazines, so you may want to look at a copy before you subscribe.

TEACHING AIDS

MOBILES: Mobiles are a nice way to display many pictures (they also keep pictures away from little brothers and sisters). Here are several kinds, ranging from simple to more complex:

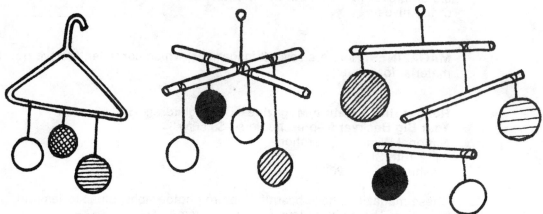

An ordinary coat hanger with yarn hanging down. This can be hung from a ceiling light or a curtain rod.

A cross made from cut pieces of clothes hanger or even soda straws. Tie it firmly in the center and hang from a light fixture or attach to ceiling with thumbtack.

The most elaborate kind is made from different length pieces of hanger, loosely joined with yarn, string or fishing line. This is the most attractive, but takes a little time juggling the ends so they'll balance evenly.

PAPER BOOKS: Children love to make little books for themselves. I take several 2" x 4" pieces of paper, fold them in half and staple the middle. On the front, I write the title (such as "My Butterfly Book"), then the children can fill them with appropriate stickers or glue in pictures. The children can also draw their own pictures on the pages, if they wish.

TISSUE PICTURES: Another fun way to make pictures or holiday decorations is with 1" squares of colored tissue paper, available at art supply or craft stores. These are held over the bottom of a pencil, dipped in glue and then pressed down on a pre-drawn outline. The steps are repeated until the picture is filled in. The children may also want to make abstract color designs.

COLLAGES: These are pictures made up of pictures or other kinds of material. For instance, when talking about fruit, the children can glue many pictures of fruit overlapping each other onto construction paper. You can also use dried beans, scraps of fabric, cotton balls—anything that can be glued down will work in a collage.

MATCHING GAMES: Make small cardboard game boards with squares for the number of different stickers that you have. Place a different sticker in each square. Mount matching stickers on small cardboard squares. The children then must place each small square over the matching square on the board.

RECIPES

Since there are a few recipes that we use a lot, I thought it would be helpful to include them here:

PLAY DOUGH

1 c. flour
½ c. salt
1 c. water
1 T. oil
1 T. alum
2 T. vanilla
food coloring

Mix dry ingredients. Add oil, water and coloring. Cook over medium heat, stirring constantly until it reaches the consistency of mashed potatoes. Remove from heat. Add vanilla. This will store for about a month, if kept sealed inside a plastic bag or other airtight container.

COOKIE DOUGH

1 c. margarine
1 ½ c. sugar
2 eggs
1 T. orange juice
1 T. orange rind, optional
1 t. vanilla
½ t. soda
½ t. salt
4-5 c. flour

Cream margarine and sugar; beat in eggs. Sift together dry ingredients and add to creamed mixture. Add rind, juice and vanilla. Chill. This keeps a long time in the refrigerator, or divide into fourths, place in plastic wrap and freeze. (This way you can thaw just what you need at one time.) When ready, bake at 350 degrees for 8 minutes.

SOFT PRETZELS

¾ c. warm water
1 pkg. dry yeast
½ t. salt
2 c. flour
½ t. sugar
Day 2 — ½ egg, kosher salt

Add yeast to water, stirring until dissolved. Add salt, sugar; stir. Add flour; stir. Knead very lightly on floured surface until completely smooth. Store in greased container with plastic wrap on top, for at least one hour or overnight. Punch dough down. Divide into 16 equal portions. Shape into pretzels (or whatever shape you are talking about that day) and place on an aluminum foil-lined cookie sheet. Brush with egg, sprinkle lightly with kosher salt. Bake at 425 degrees for 15 minutes.

FINALLY

Here are just a few hints to help things run more smoothly for you:

1. Relax: remember that the purpose of this book is not to push your child into doing things he isn't ready for. Let him learn new concepts when *he*'s ready.

2. Be Flexible: if you're about to study winter and the days are balmy and warm, substitute another unit (unless, of course, your winters are always balmy and warm!).

3. Be Patient: especially the first month, you'll find your child's attention span will probably be quite short—a five- to ten-minute lesson and a ten-minute craft may be enough. By the end of the year, the children usually want things to go on all day!

4. Avoid Distractions: it is terribly frustrating for both your child and you to have phone interruptions, etc. Take the phone off the hook or turn the bell down, so you can't hear it. Soon, the neighbor children will know when you cannot be disturbed.

5. Be Willing to Share: from time to time, include other children in your activities. Field trips are a good time to do this. Parties are much more fun when others are included, and there are several scheduled on days when we talk about the holidays. Be careful, however, not to include them too often—the purpose of this book is for mothers to spend time with their own children.

6. Have Fun: remember, the whole point about your time with your child is to help him love to learn, to do things, to enjoy books. Don't let the mechanics spoil that!

SUBJECT

	Monday	Wednesday	Friday
INTRODUCTION			
STORIES BOOKS			
FINGERPLAYS RECORDS SONGS			
ARTWORK CRAFTS PROJECTS			
TREATS			

CHAPTER 2
ME AND MYSELF

Begin by describing one child and letting the children guess who it is. Since we are talking about their physical bodies, this description would only involve their physical self: the color of their eyes and hair, their height, clothes they are wearing, etc. Repeat with all children.

Have a tape recording made in advance with lots of children's names on it. When they hear their name, they stand up. Then have the recording give them directions of something to do after their name, for example, "John, march around," "Jennifer, jump around."

Show pictures of each child at different ages. Children always love to talk about themselves as babies.

Have each child tell a story about himself: "Once upon a time, there was a little boy/girl named _____ who was _____ years old," etc. Help him include facts about himself, and the things he likes to do. Sometimes, it helps for you to tell a story about him first, so he understands the idea.

If he isn't already doing it, this is a good time for him to learn to write his name. Start by writing the child's name in large letters, both upper and lower case. Have him trace it several times. Then have him practice writing each letter individually. (It's more fun if the child uses a different colored crayon each time he writes a letter.)

Big, Bigger, Biggest, Edward W. Dolch
Big Beds, Little Beds, Dorothy Z. Seymour
The Birthday Party, Ruth Krauss
I'm Glad to be Me, P. K. Hallinan
A Birthday for Frances, Russell Hoban

"Happy Birthday Song"
This might be a fun time to play marching
music and then ask each child to do something
to it, according to name and age.

Today is *(child's name)* birthday.
Let's make her/him a cake.
We'll stir it and mix it *(Show stirring.)*
And then it can bake. *(Pretend to put cake into
oven.)*
Here's our cake, it looks so nice. *(Make a circle
with arms.)*
The frosting we'll put on. *(Pretend to frost
cake.)*
Then we can add *(child's age)* candles,
And sing a birthday song. *(Then pretend to
blow out candles.)*

(This can be repeated with each child.)

JACK AGE 6
HEIGHT 54"
WEIGHT 87 lbs.

Measure each child on a grow chart on the
wall. These can be homemade and colored by
the children or purchased commercially. Weigh
them, too. Write this information by their height
and mark the date. This is a fun activity to
repeat a number of times throughout the year.

LINDA
AGE 3
HEIGHT 37"
WEIGHT 45 lbs.

Make a birthday cake card for each child. Put
his name, age, height and weight on it. Have
the child color the candles and put the correct
number for his age on the cake. Display it in
his room.

Let each child color in the letters of his/her name on a piece of white paper. Then he can place the sign by different things in the house that are his.

Help the children make their initials out of pretzel or cookie dough (see recipe section). They can make some for the whole family if they would like.

DAY 2
PARTS OF MY BODY

Ask them what their "body" is. Help them understand that it is all of them from head to toe.

Put pictures of parts of the body on a board or flannel board. Ask them what they are.

Show them a doll. Have them name each part of the body as you point to it. Then have them do so on their own bodies. This is easier for them the first time if you go from head to toe: head, hair, eyes, nose, ears, mouth, chin, neck, shoulders, etc. Then repeat, calling out different parts at random.

Draw a stick figure, leaving off the head. Ask what is missing. Repeat several times, leaving off different parts.

The Very Little Boy, Phyllis Krasilovsky
About Me, Jane Moncure
The Shape of Me and Other Stuff, Dr. Seuss

"Head, Shoulders, Knees and Toes"

Hello, Harry! *(Point to hair.)*
How's Chester? *(Point to chest.)*
He just got back from the front. *(Point to their back, then front.)*
His feet were needed in the Army. *(Point to feet, knees, then arms.)*
Hip, hip, hooray!! *(hands on hips and then raised up in the air like leading a cheer)*

Point to your head. Now point to your nose.
Point to your knees. Then point to your toes.
Point to your leg. Now point to your eye.
Point to your elbow and then to your thigh.

Open, shut them; open, shut them;
Give a little clap.
Open, shut them; open, shut them;
Lay them in your lap.
Creep them, creep them.
Way up to your chin!
Open wide your mouth
But do not let them in.

Ten little fingers
Ten littles toes
Two little ears
And one little nose.
Two little eyes
One mouth
And a chin
It's a big secret,
But I'll let you in.
It's me!

Fingerprint art: This is a fun activity for children. All you need is an ink pad with washable, nontoxic ink and sheets of paper. The possibilities are endless.

Draw around each child on butcher paper; cut out. Let child color in his face and the clothes he is wearing. Hang it on display for the rest of the unit. Or cut the picture into parts like a puzzle and let the child put it together.

DAY 3
THINGS MY BODY CAN DO

Show pictures of children doing things. Ask what they are doing in each picture. Ask them what part or parts of their body they are using for each activity.

Have them do things with their bodies. Then ask them what they are using. For instance: "Jump up and down. Now what are you using?" (your legs) The children can swing their arms, wiggle their fingers and nod their heads.

Play "What do we do with it?" We hear with our _____; we see with our _____; we chew with our _____; etc. Repeat, using incorrect statements, for example, "We smell with our feet," and let them correct you.

Ask them to name the things they can do by themselves, such as wash their hands, brush their teeth, pick up toys.

Help them notice the special helpers that we have on our bodies to help us move—our joints (elbows, knees, wrists, knuckles, ankles, shoulders).

The Run, Jump, Bump Book, Robert Brooks
The Running, Jumping, Throwing, Sliding, Racing, Climbing Book, Oscar Weigle
Hop, Skip and Jump Book, Jack Kent
I Can, Can You? Ada Litchfield
Is It Hard, Is It Easy, Mary M. Greer

Make a collage of body-part pictures cut from magazines. This can include eyes, noses, mouths, hands, legs.

Have the children make a little booklet with pictures of people (preferably boys and girls) running, throwing, sleeping, and doing other things.

Make a little chart with the sun on one side and the moon on the other. Draw little stick figures of what the children tell you they do during the day.

Make a "mirror" out of cardboard for each child. The "face" can be made by gluing in aluminum foil or letting the child draw his own face. On the handle of the mirror you can put his name and age or the list of things he told you earlier that he can do by himself. This little poem can be put on the other side:

"When I look in the mirror, what do I see?
A smiling face looking back at me.
That face looks so nice.
Now who could it be?
Well, what do you know?
That face must be me!"

Make taffy and when it's cool, let the children use their arms and hands to pull and stretch it.

Make cookies and let the children use their hands and arms to roll it out. Talk about what they are doing.

DAY 4
FACIAL EXPRESSIONS

Have the children look in a mirror. What do they see? You can give them each a hand mirror or let them line up in front of a bathroom mirror or some other large mirror and look at each other, too. Have them look surprised, angry, happy, sad.

Show pictures of different things such as a birthday cake, a present, a rainy day, a dog, etc. Let the children show on their faces how each picture makes them feel. Let them again see their faces in a mirror.

Make a list drawing a happy face on one side and a sad face on the other. Ask the children to think of things that make them happy. Then ask them to think of things that make them sad.

Use a tape recorder to play back crying, yelling, laughing, giggling and other vocal sounds, and have the children tell the emotion that they hear.

Alexander and the Terrible, Horrible, No Good, Very Bad Day, Judith Viorst

If you're happy and you know it, make a grin,
If you're happy and you know it, make a grin,
If you're happy and you know it,
Then your face will surely show it,
If you're happy and you know it, make a grin.
Repeat with other verses:
"If you're sad and you know it, make a frown,"
"If you're sleepy and you know it, make a yawn,"
"If you're angry and you know it, make a scowl," etc.

Make a happy-frowny face on a paper plate. Holding the plate up to their faces, the children can dance around, changing the face and their actions accordingly.

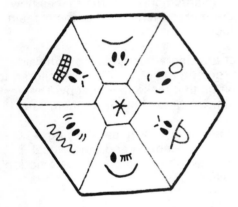

Let each child make and color a "Face Game" to play. Insert a short pencil through the center. Spin it like a top and take turns imitating the facial expression shown when it stops.

Bake pre-made, round sugar cookies. Let the children frost them and put different faces on them with cinnamon candies or raisins.

DAY 5
MY SENSES

Show pictures of ears, nose, mouth, hands and eyes. Let the children talk about what each can do.

Have little bags or boxes prepared ahead of time for each sense. Blindfold them (except for the "eyes" bag), and let them guess what each thing is.

Hearing: Rattle, bell, watch or clock, aluminum foil to crush or rattle, seeds or beans in a box to shake.

Smell: Orange, banana, a match after the flame has been blown out, vanilla, perfume, flower, pine (candle or scent).

Taste: Apple, peppermint candy, licorice, lemon, pickle, salt, sugar, ice cream or something cold, cocoa or something warm.

Touch: Piece of velvet or fur cloth, round rubber ball, sand, sticky tape, ice, sandpaper, a glass surface (mirror or bottle).

Sight: Picture of a rainbow or a butterfly, things to view through a piece of colored glass or colored cellophane, a magnifying glass to look at their skin.

Tape record sounds and see if they can name what they hear: running water, emptying ice from an ice tray, opening the refrigerator door, the doorbell.

Five Senses, Tasha Tudor
Do You Know What I Know? Helen Borton
Listen! Listen! Ylla
Hailstones and Halibut Bones, Mary O'Neill

My tongue can taste.
My eyes can see.
My nose can smell wherever I may be.
My fingers touch.
My ears can hear.
My body lets me know about whatever may appear.

(Point to each as you talk about it.)

Have the children glue pictures of eyes, ears, nose and mouth onto a round circle face or paper plate, putting them where they belong.

Make up little cards with eyes, ears, noses, mouths and hands on them. Let the children color them if you wish. The children can then play a game by drawing a card and naming something that they can see, smell, etc., with that sense.

Let the children have some of the food that they previously tasted or smelled.

DAY 6
CLOTHES

Show pictures of different articles of clothing. Let them name each one. (Catalogs are great sources for these.)

Pull clothing out of a large bag and let the child or children put each piece on. This is especially fun if you put in Daddy's big boots, a costume clown hat, Mommy's gloves, and other articles of clothing that they would not ordinarily wear.

Talk about the different kinds of clothes we wear depending upon the weather—jackets, snow pants, hats and gloves in winter; shorts, swimsuits in summer, etc. Talk about what kinds of clothes we wear at different times of the day — pajamas or nightgowns at night, play clothes for outside with friends, special clothes for church or parties.

Talk about each part of the body and what we wear on it: head — hat or earmuffs; hands — gloves or mittens; body — shirt or blouse, sweater or jacket; legs — pants or skirt; feet — socks, shoes, slippers or boots. They can make-believe they are putting on the different articles of clothing as you talk about them.

New Shoes, Sam Vaughn
Little Black Sambo, Helen Bannerman

Glue clothes cut from fabric onto a paper person.

Make and color paper dolls with clothes and play with them.

Make cookies, cutting the dough into shapes of boots, hats, coats, pants, etc.

CHAPTER 3
FAMILIES

DAY 1	**WHO IS IN MY FAMILY?**
DAY 2	**WHAT FAMILY MEMBERS DO**
DAY 3	**WHO ARE MY RELATIVES?**

DAY 1
WHO IS IN MY FAMILY?

Describe individual family members. Let them guess who you are talking about.

Display different pictures of people of varying ages. (An old catalog or magazine can be an excellent source for these pictures.) Let the children identify which look like mothers, which look like fathers, etc. This can be fun if they glue or stick them onto a chart with all the mothers together, all the sisters, etc.

Show pictures of family members at different ages. When a boy sees his father at his age, it helps him realize that he can someday be a daddy, too.

Be sure to help the children understand that every family is different: some have no daddy or mommy, some have no sisters or brothers, etc. Help them understand that although each family is different, families are special because of the love that they have for one another.

Are You My Mother? P.D. Eastman
Wanted . . . a Brother, Gina Bell
Father is Big, Ruth Radlauer
Big Brother, Charlotte Zolotow

See my family, see them all. *(Hold up five fingers.)*
Some are short, *(thumb up)*
And some are tall.*(middle finger up)*
Let's shake hands—"How do you do?" *(Clasp hands and shake.)*
See them bow—"And how are you?"*(Bend fingers.)*
Father, *(middle finger)*
Mother, *(pointer finger)*
Sister, *(ring finger)*
Brother, *(thumb)*
And me, *(little finger)*
Together we're a family.

Make little stick puppets of family members on tongue depressors or Popsicle sticks. These can be catalog pictures that the children think look like their family, or the children can draw them on themselves. Mount them on cardboard, so they'll stay rigid before gluing to the sticks. The children can make up a little play with the family members talking to one another.

Make a family mobile using directions in Chapter 1. Copy enough pictures for each family member. You can change the hair and coloring to adapt to each family member.

Provide the children with large and small marshmallows and toothpicks. Let them make marshmallow people of their family. They can save them to show the rest of the family at dinner, or they can eat them, when they're done.

Hold up a picture of a father or their own father and ask the children what he does. Discuss not only what kind of work he does outside the home, but also talk about what he does to help around the house. Repeat for each member of the family.

Have them pantomime the things that each family member does. Especially talk about the chores that they do around the house in order to lead up to the activities for this day.

Let the children dress up in some of the other family members' clothes. Talk about how they feel when they are dressed that way. Again they could act out what the member does. (Be sure you clear this with the clothes' owners first!)

A Father Like That, Charlotte Zolotow
Just Me and My Dad, Mercer Mayer
The Way Mothers Are, Miriam Schlein
Big Sister, Little Sister, Charlotte Zolotow

Let the children make a coupon(s) for each family member promising to do something to help them. Perhaps they can polish Daddy's shoes (with your supervision, of course!), clean the table for Mommy, empty the garbage for brother, sort sister's hair ribbons, or play with the baby. If possible, let them think of their own ideas.

Make family paper dolls, one for each member of your family. Let the children color in clothes, add facial features.

Have them do a good deed for each family member (things like making brother's bed, drawing a picture, straightening shoes in the closet, helping put laundry away). Have them ask the family at dinner to guess what they did for each of them today.

Let the children decorate a cookie for each family member to share with them at dinner. They can be decorated with frosting or colored sprinkles.

DAY 3
WHO ARE MY RELATIVES?

Show pictures of a grandfather and a grandmother. Help the children understand who grandparents are.

Show pictures of *their* grandparents. It is especially important if the grandparents are no longer living for the child to understand who they are. Children need to know that they still had grandparents, even if they are no longer alive.

If possible, show photographs of yourself as a child with your parents. Help the children understand who their grandparents are in relation to them.

Talk about things that grandparents do. If they live in different cities and the child doesn't visit with them frequently, talk about the things that their grandparents do each day and things that they do where they live.

Now is a good time, if the child is not as close to one set of grandparents as the other, to help him know more about both sets—make sure you give them all equal time!

Help them understand that their aunts and uncles are your brothers and sisters, just as they or their friends have brothers and sisters.

Grandmother Lucy Books, Joyce Wood
Mary Jo's Grandmother, Janice M. Udry
Grandpa's Long Red Underwear, Lynn
 Schoettle
Grandmother Told Me, Jan Wahl

These are grandmother's glasses. *(Make round circles with fingers.)*
This is grandmother's cap. *(Place hand on top of head.)*
This is the way she folds her hands. *(Fold hands in air.)*
And puts them in her lap. *(Rest hands in lap.)*

Have the children draw a picture or dictate a letter to send to their grandparents.

Have the children decorate a cardboard frame. Place a snapshot of the children inside, and give to the grandparents.

If grandparents live close by, a visit can be arranged to their home this day.

CHAPTER 4
HOMES

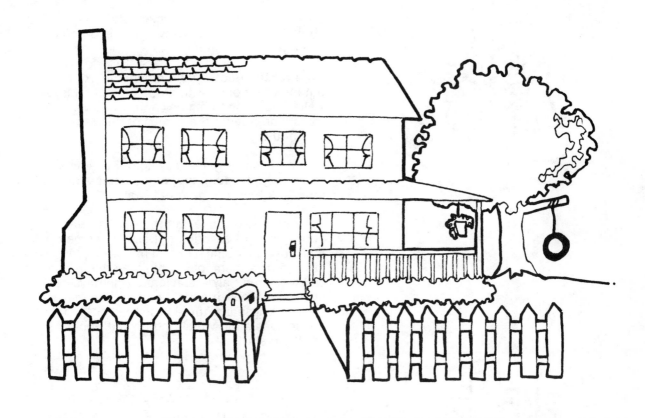

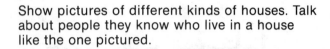

Show pictures of different kinds of houses. Talk about people they know who live in a house like the one pictured.

On a piece of construction paper, make the outline of a house with strips of paper. Make walls, roof, door, chimney and windows. Help the children learn the names of different parts of a house.

Play a guessing game, saying, for example, "People go through me to get inside a house" (door); "I hold up the roof" (walls).

Describe their house. Let them guess whose house you are describing. Describe some of their friends' homes. Let them guess. (You may have to give them lots of hints on this, since children aren't always aware of the physical features of their friends' houses.) You may say, "In this house live three brothers" or "In this house lives a big white dog named Sugar," to get them started.

My House, Miriam Schlein
What is a House? Richard Scarry
A House for Everyone, Betty Miles

There's a little round house
With a little yellow roof.
And two windows upstairs to look out.
There's a latch to loose
And a little red door
To walk inside no doubt.

(Child's name) head is the little house.
His golden hair is the roof.
His eyes are the upstairs windows.
His nose is the latch to loose.
And what do you think is the little door?
Why *(child's name)* mouth, of course!

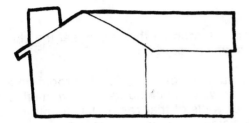

Draw the outline of a house in black on a piece of paper. Let the children color it in.

On colored construction paper, let the children glue toothpicks to make a house form.

Make a little house booklet to be used for the whole unit. Enlarge the picture onto the lower half of an 8x10 piece of paper. Fold in half on the roof line. This is the cover. The children can color these today. (You can either leave the outside margin of the piece of paper as it is or actually cut around it, so that the book looks like a house.) On subsequent days, you will add colored paper to match the different rooms in your house. These pages can be stapled together along the roof line, or yarn can be threaded through two holes punched along the top.

With carrot and celery sticks, let the children form a house on a plate, before eating it!

Describe a room in the house. Let the children guess which room it is.

Put up a piece of paper for that room on a chart or wall, matching its color with either the floor or walls of that room. (It's helpful to use these same colors in the booklet.)

Talk about what each room is used for. Pantomime what we do in each room. The children might even want to pantomime how we clean each room: vacuum, scrub the floor, etc.

Tell them you are going to talk about the things we do in each room, but that you will mix them all up. Say, for example, "We sleep in the kitchen," "We take baths in the living room," and let the children correct you.

This might be a good time to review any rules that you might have for your house, such as not running inside, only eating in the kitchen, etc. (whatever the rules are in your house!).

A Place to Stay, Frank Jupo
The Little House, Virginia Burton
A Little House of Your Own, Beatrice
    DeRegniers & Irene Haas

I have a nice house.
Here is the floor *(Hold palms out flat.)*
Here are the walls, *(Intertwine fingers together.)*
The roof, *(Place fingertips together.)*
And the door. *(Hold hands open and then clap together.)*

Let the children choose something to make or do for a room in the house, such as pick flowers for a vase, or draw a picture for the wall.

Make the room pages for your house booklet. Write down the name of the room at the bottom of each page.

DAY 3
FURNITURE

Show pictures of different pieces of furniture cut from a magazine or catalog. After you have talked about each piece, have the children glue it to the chart you made on Day 2, placing it in the correct room.

Describe a piece of furniture. Let them guess what it is.

Talk about the different parts of a piece of furniture. For instance, on a chair, show the back, the legs, the seat. (Use dollhouse furniture or the furniture in your home.)

Place doll furniture or pictures in a bag. As the children remove them one at a time, let them tell what each is and where it goes.

Have them pantomime being a piece of furniture: a chair, a table, a bed. Kids really love this if you help them get started.

Goldilocks and the Three Bears
At Our House, Lois Lenski
A People House, Theo. LeSeig

From the pictures that the children have seen, let them choose furniture that they like and glue them to a piece of paper.

Let the children choose from pictures all the furniture that goes in the same room and glue to a piece of paper.

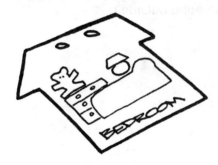

Glue or color pictures of furniture in the little rooms in your house booklet.

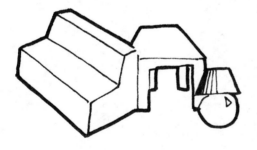

Out of lightweight cardboard or heavy paper, make little pieces of furniture. These can be painted or colored before assembly.

DAY 4
HOW A HOUSE IS BUILT

Talk about some of the things that houses are made of and possibly have things to show them, such as a brick, a large rock, wood.

Discuss tools used in building. Let the children hammer nails into a board, use sandpaper, pliers.

Bring toy trucks like those used in construction. Talk about what they do. (If the weather permits, and you have a sand pile, this could be done outside.)

The Biggest House in the World, Leo Leonni
Around the House that Jack Built, Roz Abisch

I'll take a hammer and rap, rap, rap. *(Make fist with one hand and pound in palm of other.)*
With a saw I'll see, saw, see, *(Pretend to be sawing.)*
And now with a brush, I can paint, paint, paint, *(Pretend to be painting.)*
To build a house for me.

44

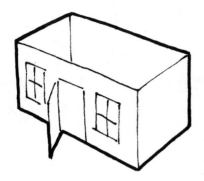

Make a little house from a cardboard box. Place carpet scraps inside. Use old wallpaper for walls. Cut door and windows. Put in furniture you made in Day 3.

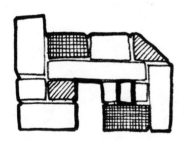

Build a house with wood blocks or plastic building bricks.

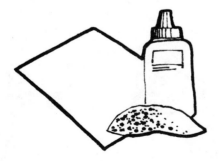

Make a sawdust picture, mixing sawdust (available from a lumber store) with dry tempera to create colors. Make design with glue; sprinkle sawdust on as desired; blow excess off when dry.

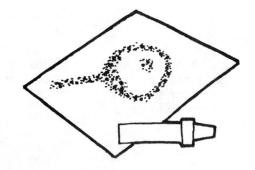

Make a sandpaper picture: with crayons, color a picture onto a large piece of sandpaper. Place a piece of paper toweling over the picture and iron at a low setting to set the picture.

Visit a construction site to watch the workmen at their tasks. Talk about what is going on.

Build little houses out of graham crackers and frosting or make a little gingerbread house. (These can be done for any day in this unit.)

Show pictures of homes from other lands: igloo, grass hut, stilt house, chalet. Encyclopedias are good sources for these pictures. Ask them what they think it would be like living in these kinds of homes. What kinds of clothes would they have to wear in homes like these? How would they take care of these homes?

Show pictures of apartments, house trailers, duplexes or other multi-family dwellings. Talk about how they are different from your home. (Of course, if you live in one of these homes, you need to approach this differently!) Help the children understand that it doesn't matter what kind of house someone lives in: it is still "home" to him.

Have You Seen Houses? Joanne Oppenheim
Houses Around the World, Louise L. Floethe
Alfred Goes House Hunting, Bill Binzen
We Live by the River, Lois Lenski
We Live in the City, Lois Lenski

Arrange a visit inside an apartment, trailer or some other kind of home than the one you live in. Talk to the owners about why they like their house.

Take a drive in your car and talk about all the kinds of homes you see.

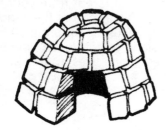

Build an igloo out of sugar cubes and frosting "glue."

Make an Eskimo igloo cake: cut two layer cakes in half; frost three half-layers with white frosting and set all four side-by-side on a plate; frost the outside edges. With melted chocolate or colored frosting draw the ice blocks onto the white frosting. If you want, you can use a cut-down cupcake for the entrance tunnel. This is fun to make during the day and serve to the whole family that night.

Talk about the different kinds of homes that animals have, such as a beaver dam, a bear's cave, a bird's nest and a rabbit's burrow.

Talk about why they have that kind of home and how they make it.

Put a blanket or sheet over a table and have the children pretend that they are little bears in a cave or bunnies in a burrow. Let them think how they would feel in this kind of home. Ask them what they would like about it and what they wouldn't like.

The Brownstone, Paula Scher
The Beaver's Home, Alvin Tresselt
Pippa Mouse, Betty Boegehold

A cave is nice for a big brown bear. *(Put arms in a circle.)*
A bird lives in the tree. *(Hook thumbs, flap outstretched fingers.)*
A hive is the very nicest home
For a happy little bee. *(Cup hands together.)*

Here is a nest for the robin. *(Cup hands.)*
Here is the hive for the bee *(Place fists together.)*
Here is a hole for the bunny, *(fingers and thumb together to make a circle)*
And here is a house for me! *(fingertips together to make a roof)*

With playdough (see recipes—Chapter 1) or clay, make different kinds of animals' homes.

With sticks and clay, let the children build a play beaver's dam or bird's nest.

CHAPTER 5
FALL

DAY 1
WHAT IS FALL?

Tell a story about a green leaf changing colors and finally falling off. This can be drawn or told with flannel board pictures.

Show a pine tree branch. Talk about its "leaves"— the needles. Talk about why they don't fall off. (When you go for your autumn walk, point out various evergreens.)

Talk about the weather in the fall—some days, it's cool, and some days, it's hot. Explain that the cool weather tells the animals and plants that it's time to get ready for winter. The leaves on the trees start to change color and fall. The birds fly south and the squirrels gather food.

Cut leaf shapes out of colored paper and let the children match them with pieces of colored construction paper. Have them name the colors.

Now It's Fall, Lois Lenski
Follow the Fall, Maxine Kumin
A Pocketful of Season, Doris Foster
The Bears' Almanac, Stan and Jan Berenstain,
    pp. 54-57

I like leaves, all kinds of leaves.
Bright little red leaves,
Quiet little brown leaves,
Happy little green leaves,
Sunny little yellow leaves.
I like leaves, all kinds of leaves.

(*Have the children hold up the matching leaf as you talk about each color.*)

Rake leaves into a big pile outside and have the children run and jump into them.

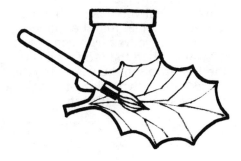

Paint leaves with tempera paints (you may have to press them first with an iron on a low setting). Glue onto a piece of paper.

Paint with pine needles or use a whole branch as a brush.

Go for a walk. Have the children collect a bag of different colored leaves for Day 2's activities. You can also make this into a scavenger hunt by asking them to collect certain things that are symbols of fall, such as acorns, colored leaves, seeds, pinecones, nuts and cocoons (you will want to have them just show you these).

Draw a large picture of a tree on newsprint and tape to the wall. Have the children glue or tape leaves to it.

Have the children look at the leaves you gathered. Have them make a pile of each color. Let the children count the leaves and match the shapes.

Have the children look at the veins in the leaves. (This works best with leaves that are not very dried out.) Explain that the food for the tree is made in the leaves by mixing sunshine and water. Then the food travels to the rest of the tree through the veins. Tell them that these are like their own veins—the ones at their wrists are the easiest to identify.

Johnny Maple Leaf, Alvin Tresselt
All Falling Down, Gene Zion

See the bright leaves on the trees, *(Pretend to be trees.)*
Rustling in the autumn breeze, *(Wave their arms back and forth.)*
Whirling, twirling through the air, *(Turn around like leaves.)*
Fall here and there. *(Fall on the floor.)*

Have the children pretend that they are leaves and dance to music.

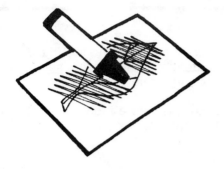

Make leaf rubbings from your collected leaves: put a leaf under a piece of paper; rub over the paper with a side of a crayon, until an imprint comes through. Several can be done on one piece of paper using different shaped leaves and different colored crayons.

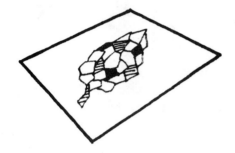

Make a collage of leaves on a piece of construction paper.

Make a leaf mobile (see Chapter 1): cut different shaped leaves out of colored construction paper, or use white paper and have the children color them. They are extra pretty if you glue matching-colored pipe cleaners around the outside of each leaf.

Talk about and then eat edible leaves, such as lettuce, spinach and cabbage.

DAY 3
WHAT DO PEOPLE AND ANIMALS DO IN THE FALL?

Show pictures of animals who live in places that have winter as a cold season, such as bears, rabbits, squirrels and insects.

Talk about how they store food and dig homes in the ground, their fur gets heavier, bears eat a lot.

Talk about what people do: harvest their crops, protect their plants, rake the leaves, clean their gardens—whatever you do.

The Tale of the Grasshopper and the Ant
   (various authors)
The Tale of Squirrel Nutkin, Beatrix Potter
Where Does Everyone Go? Aileen Fisher
Sleepy Time, Eva Evans
Wake Up Groundhog! Carol Cohen

When autumn comes, it's a special time
Our yard we clean and rake. *(Show cleaning and raking.)*
We gather all the leaves around, *(Make a big circle with arms.)*
And a great big pile we make—jump! *(On the word* jump, *pretend to jump into a pile of leaves.)*

Have the children color outlines of tree trunks brown and then glue little torn-tissue colored "leaves" on them (see Chapter 1 for tissue pictures).

Make a little weather chart, where they can keep track of the weather for this week or several weeks. This will help them be aware of the changing fall weather.

Have hot or cold apple cider or apple juice.

CHAPTER 6
FOOD AND HARVEST

Show an orange, apple, banana or other fruit (you can use pictures if you want). Have the children identify them.

Put the fruit into a bag and let the children guess what each is by feeling it.

Talk about how each fruit is different. An apple has a smooth skin that can be eaten; if you cut one in half cross-wise, the children can see the little star made by the seeds in the center. An orange skin has more little bumps on it and has to be peeled before you can eat the fruit. A banana has to be peeled, too, and the seeds are so little they can be eaten. (You might want to put a banana in the refrigerator for a few days until the skin turns black, but—surprise!— the inside is still perfect for eating.) Discuss other fruit as you wish.

Talk about the fact that not all fruit grows on trees. Berries and pineapple grow on bushes, and melons and grapes grow on vines.

Blueberries for Sal, Robert McCloskey
Who's Got the Apple, Jan Loot
The Beetle Bush, (watermelon), Beverly Keller
An Apple a Day, Judith Barrett
Good Lemonade, Frank Asch
The Blueberry Pie Elf, Catherine Wooley

Have the children match all the pictures of fruit that are red; then yellow; then purple; then green; then orange. If you want, they can be glued on separate pages and made into a book.

Visit a farmer's market and see all the fruit (and other food on display).

Visit a cider mill or apple orchard.

Make a fruit salad using as many fresh fruits as you can.

Have cider or apple juice.

Repeat Day 1, using vegetables; have them identify different vegetables either by taste or by touch.

Talk about the way vegetables grow: some are called "root" vegetables, such as carrots, radishes, turnips and beets—because they grow underground. Others grow on bushes or vines, such as beans, peas, and cucumbers. Others are nearly the whole plant, such as cabbages, cauliflower, spinach and lettuce. Some are called "leafy" vegetables, such as lettuce and spinach.

Let the children break beans into pieces for cooking, open pea pods to remove the peas, or husk corn.

Match vegetables by color, just as you did with fruit.

Lentil Soup, Joe Laski
Blue Bug's Vegetable Garden, Virginia Poulet
The Turnip, A. Tolstoy
Autumn Harvest, Alvin Tresselt

Do vegetable printing: cut the ends off of various hard vegetables, such as carrots, celery and radishes. Press against a sponge saturated with tempera paint. Stamp a design onto paper. You can also carefully cut a design into the end of the vegetable, which can be stamped onto paper. (A stamp pad can also be used instead of the paint and the sponge.)

Paint a picture with a celery stalk and tempera, using the leaves as bristles. The painting won't look great, but it's lots of fun.

Make a vegetable man out of colored construction paper: a tomato for a head, a potato for a body, pea pods for arms, carrots for legs and radishes for feet.

Cut up vegetables and make vegetable soup, using tomato juice or broth for the liquid.

Cut the vegetables into different shapes for the children to eat: carrot "pennies," celery "moons," broccoli "trees," radish "flowers."

Show a picture of a cow—explain that milk comes from a cow. The children can pretend that they are milking a cow. Tell them what happens to the milk after it leaves the cow: it is pasteurized and placed in sterilized containers; then it is sent to the store or the milkman delivers it to your door.

Show pictures of different dairy products and explain how they are made. *Cheese* is made by letting the milk sour until it comes together in solid pieces called curds. The liquid is drained off and the curds pressed together to form the cheese. *Butter* is made by mixing or shaking cream until the fat comes together and forms butter. *Ice cream* is made by putting cream, sugar and eggs in a freezer. Nuts or fruit can be added, too. The freezer is placed inside a bucket filled with ice and salt. Then a crank turns a paddle inside the freezer so that the mixture freezes evenly. (NOTE: This information may be a little beyond the understanding of most preschoolers, so don't feel you have to explain unless the child asks.)

Some Cheese for Charles, Helen Buckley
The Land Where the Ice Cream Grows,
   Anthony Burgess

Visit a dairy and watch the cows being milked and the milk containers being filled.

Whip cream until it turns into butter (the kids love this!).

Make homemade ice cream.

Any dairy product is appropriate for this day. If you have whipped cream into butter, that would be especially fun for them to try on bread.

DAY 4
MEAT

Show pictures of different animals and discuss the meat that we get from them: cattle—hamburger, hot dogs, steak; sheep—lamb or mutton; pig—pork, bacon, ham; poultry—chicken, turkey.

Hold up the animal's picture and have the children tell you what we get from this animal.

Show pictures of different cuts of meat and talk about how we eat them. They can pretend that they are frying the hamburger, basting the turkey, etc.

Also, explain that we get eggs from chickens. Talk about all the different ways that we can cook eggs.

Mother Rabbit's Son, Tom (about a rabbit who wants to eat hamburgers, instead of carrots), Dick Gackenbach
The Egg Book, Jack Kent
EAT, Diane Peterson
Green Eggs and Ham, Dr. Seuss

Visit a butcher shop and have the butcher show the children how he cuts the big pieces of meat into different sizes.

Visit the meat department of your grocery store and talk about all the different kinds of meat.

Make hot dog racers for lunch: place heated hot dog in a bun; add four carrot "wheels" attached with toothpicks and an olive "driver."

DAY 5
GRAINS

Show pictures of wheat or kernels of actual wheat. Let the children pretend that they are grinding the wheat to make flour and then making bread.

Talk about other kinds of grains and how we eat them: oatmeal—cereal, cookies, etc.; rice—cooked, puddings, etc.; corn—tortillas, cornbread; rye—bread.

The Little Red Hen (various authors)
Bread and Jam for Frances, Russell Hoban
The Giant Jam Sandwich, John Lord and Janet
   Burroway
Clabber Biscuits, Ida Chittum
The Sandwich, Dorothy Seymour

Make a collage of dried beans, wheat, rice and other grains. This can be done by drawing a picture on a piece of cardboard that the children can glue the pieces of grain onto, or letting them just make up their own designs.

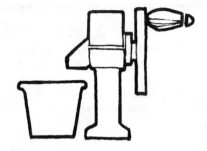

Grind wheat into flour. A food processor will do this if you don't have a grinder.

Make bread or little muffins with the wheat that you have ground.

Break off little pieces of thawed frozen bread dough or homemade bread dough. Roll flat and fry until light brown. Serve with butter and jam.

Fry wheat kernels in oil until just brown. Serve salted.

Pour water into a glass; let the children taste it, feel it, smell it, color it, flavor it.

Show ice cubes and explain that they are frozen water. Put one in a saucepan and watch it turn back to water.

Fill a saucepan with boiling water. Put on the lid for a few minutes until it is covered with drops of water. Explain that when the water becomes hot, it turns to steam. This is called *evaporation*.

Fill a sponge with water; let the children squeeze it out and then soak the water back up again.

Have the children take a "colored" bath: put 6-8 drops of food coloring into the bath water. This won't color the children, but will make the bath more fun.

Put food coloring into different cups of water; mix them one with another to show new colors.

Paint on the sidewalk, using a wide brush and water. The designs will stay until they evaporate away. (This is fun in the summer, too.)

Have the children help you mix powdered drink with water. Pour into ice cube trays and freeze with toothpick handles.

Crush ice and pour punch or fruit juice over for a "snow cone."

CHAPTER 7
HALLOWEEN

DAY 1
WHAT IS HALLOWEEN?

Talk about how Halloween came about: October 31 was the last day of the year in ancient Britain, and it was celebrated as we celebrate New Year's Eve. Witches, ghosts and other eerie creatures were supposed to be about, too. The next day was a religious holiday, so the spooks only had until midnight to play.

Especially for young children, Halloween, with all the scary masks and costumes, can be a very frightening experience. It is important to talk to them about the fact that this is all make-believe and not real.

Show a set of commercial Halloween decorations. (Hallmark and other card companies make nice ones.) Talk about the characters in the pictures.

Draw a ghost face on a white balloon or piece of white cloth draped over your hand and let him talk to the children.

Dramatize riding a broom like witches. (This is also fun done to music on Day 2.)

Georgie and **Georgie's Halloween,** Robert Bright
Witch in the House, Ruth Chew
Suppose You Met a Witch, Ian Serraibbier
Clifford's Halloween, Norman Bridwell

"Danse Macabre" by Saint-Saëns is fun music to dance to. The children can pretend that they are witches, skeletons and ghosts. My children also like to put sheets on their heads and pretend that they are ghosts this way, too.

Make a matching game with Halloween stickers (see Chapter 1).

Make ghost faces on white balloons with black felt markers or make jack o'lantern faces on orange balloons.

Make and frost pumpkin cookies using raisins or small candies to make features.

Talk about the difference between a pumpkin and a jack o'lantern.

Cut out orange paper circles; leave some plain and draw jack o'lantern faces on others. Hold them up one at a time and have the children tell which are pumpkins and which are jack o'lanterns.

Make a jack o'lantern puppet by stuffing a brown paper bag and drawing on features. When the features are all drawn on, you can have the puppet "talk" to the children.

Put a cloth pumpkin on the flannel board. Let the children put on different faces from many features that you have cut out.

It's the Great Pumpkin, Charlie Brown, Charles M. Schulz
How Spider Saved Halloween, Robert Krauss

Peter, Peter, Pumpkin Eater
Had a wife and couldn't keep her,
Put her in a pumpkin shell
And there he kept her very well.

Five little pumpkins sitting on a gate.
The first one said, "Oh, my, it's getting late!"
The second one said, "There are witches in the air!"
The third one said, "I don't care!"
The fourth one said, "Let's run and run and run!"
The fifth one said, "I'm having lots of fun!"
"Woooo," went the wind.
Out went the light.
And the five little pumpkins rolled out of sight.

Go to a farm or store and buy a pumpkin. Bring it back home and carve it. (If you don't have a lot of time, this could be done ahead and just the carving could take place this day.)

Make jack o'lantern puppets, using tongue depressors with orange paper circles on the top.

Make and frost pumpkin cupcakes.

Make a pumpkin pie or pumpkin bread.

DAY 3
LET'S HAVE A HALLOWEEN PARTY

This is an especially fun day to invite friends to join you.

Decorate trick-or-treat bags using empty brown grocery bags.

Have the children decorate the room with black-and-orange paper chains.

Make sucker ghosts by covering a round sucker with a white facial tissue. Tie with a thread and draw on eyes.

Play "Pin the Tail on the Black Cat" or "Pin the Nose on the Pumpkin," by drawing a large tailless cat or orange pumpkin on construction paper and hanging it on the wall.

Let the children decorate pumpkin nut cups for the party table.

Witch, Goblin and Sometimes Ghost, Sue
　Alexander
The Old Witch's Party, Ida Delage
The Halloween Party, Lonzo Anderson

Make Halloween ghoul pictures by folding construction paper in half and dropping blobs of tempera paint down the center fold and pressing flat. Open up and let dry. Add eyes and mouth to the finished ghoul.

Make springy witches out of egg carton cups. Cut a black body and hat and a white head out of construction paper, as shown. Draw on an ugly face. Fold white paper strips in an accordion manner, and glue to body for arms and legs. Add paper hands and feet.

In our family we have always had a lot of fun making our own costumes. Sack costumes are easy to make and very versatile. Fold two yards of material in half and sew side seams, cut two leg holes on the fold side; sew a large seam or cut slits along the top edge to run ribbon cording through. A red bag can be an apple or tomato; an orange one, a pumpkin; a green one, a monster from outer space; a white one, a rabbit, a snowman or a mouse; a brown one, a dog or a monkey. All you have to do is stuff the bag with paper and add a mask, a mop-head wig dyed a matching color or ears.

A black garbage bag, cut down to fit the child, adding arm and neck holes, can make a great skeleton costume. Add the "bones" from white contact paper or tape and make the skull mask from a paper plate.

Halloween Makeup:
1 T. white shortening
2 T. cornstarch
1 tsp. white flour
4-5 drops food coloring
Mix together, adding more shortening if necessary (One T. mixed with 2½ t. cocoa makes a great brown, too.)

Orange Jello

Orange juice or orange punch

Licorice

Make a ghost cake using a cake baked in a 9x13 pan. For eyes, use Necco candy inside empty eggshell halves. Licorice string makes the mouth.

CHAPTER 8
BIRDS

DAY 1
WHAT IS A BIRD?

Show pictures of different kinds of birds. An encyclopedia or bird book from the library works well for this. Talk about the birds:

Feathers: Show one and let them feel it tickle; talk about how it helps the bird fly; how the feathers are fluffed out in the winter time to keep the bird warm; how water-birds' feathers are waterproof.

Bill: Talk about how the kind of bill a bird has helps it eat its food—a woodpecker has to have a sharp bill to peck at trees and get out insects; a pelican has a large bill that acts like a giant scoop to pick fish up from the water; a hummingbird has a needle-like bill to suck the nectar out of flowers.

Feet: Talk about how some birds, such as eagles and hawks, have claws to help them catch their prey, and others, such as ducks and other water birds, have to have webbed feet to help them move through water.

Tail: Talk about how some birds have long tails which help them perch, some have fancy tails, such as peacocks, and some have short little tails such as penguins. Let them pick the different kinds from the pictures you show them.

Talk about the different kinds of food that birds eat: some birds like insects and worms, some like seeds, some like the nectar of flowers, some eat small animals such as mice.

Talk about what birds do in the winter, such as fly south and change their eating habits.

Recipes for the Birds, Irene and Ed Cosgrove
The Early Bird, Richard Scarry
Birds, Jane Werner Watson (a Little Golden book)
Flap Your Wings, P. D. Eastman
The Bears' Nature Guide, Stan and Jan Berenstain, pp. 30-33.

Two little black birds sitting on a hill.
One named Jack and the other named Jill.
Fly away, Jack. Fly away, Jill.
Come back, Jack. Come back, Jill.

(This is fun to act out by putting two little paper birds on each index finger. Let them "fly away" behind your back and then come back.)

Roll pinecones in peanut butter or melted suet; then roll in bird seed. Hang on a branch with yarn.

Paint with a feather.

Have the children color drawings of different birds. (These can be traced from bird books.)

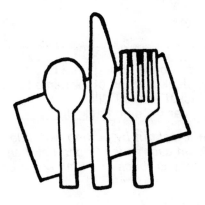

Eat toasted sunflower seeds. The children can pretend that they are birds while they do this.

Make little birds out of dough—either bread or roll dough works well. Cut strips 1"x10" and tie in a knot. Place on a cookie sheet in shape shown, squeezing the top to look like a beak. Add a raisin eye. Bake at 375 degrees until browned.

Show pictures of bird nests.

Show grass, twigs, string and other nest materials. Talk about how birds weave these together to make their nests.

If possible, show an old nest saved from last summer. If you live in an area with a lot of birds, old nests are quite easy to find in the late fall when the leaves have fallen from the trees.

Make a "nest" out of blankets. Have the children pretend that they are the baby birds in the nest. Have them fly away when they think that they are big enough.

The Best Nest, P. D. Eastman
The Nest Book, Kathleen Daly

Kookaburra sits in the old gum tree,
Eating all the gum drops that he can see.
Laugh, kookaburra, laugh, kookaburra,
Save some of them for me.

Spread puffed rice cakes (purchased in health food or Oriental grocery stores) with peanut butter. Hang these for the birds. (You'll probably find that your children love these, too!)

Make a nest plaque: glue a large empty walnut shell to a piece of old wood or shingle; glue several pinto or navy beans inside to look like eggs; florist moss can be glued around it for greenery.

Make Rice Krispy treats, but, instead of pressing the mixture into a pan to set up, let it cool a little and shape into little birds' nests.

Make cookie nests from a macaroon recipe. Here's one that I use:

3 c. coconut
⅓ c. sifted flour
⅔ c. sugar
½ t. baking powder
2 egg whites
¼ t. almond extract

Combine coconut, ⅓ c. sugar and one of the egg whites and cook, stirring constantly, over low heat till the mixture is hot. Stir in extract and flour. Beat remaining egg white till soft peaks form; gradually add remaining ⅓ c. sugar, beating until stiff peaks form. Fold into coconut mixture. Moisten hands with water; shape into 12 balls. Place on greased cookie sheet. Make an indentation in middle to form "nest." Bake at 300 degrees for 20 minutes; cool on cookie sheet 2-3 minutes before removing.

DAY 3
EGGS

Tell the story of an egg hatching. Help the children understand that the egg is formed inside the mother with the future baby inside. But instead of continuing to grow inside its mother like a human baby, the bird will grow inside the egg. Help them understand that the baby must be kept warm, so the birds take turns sitting on the eggs until the baby bird is ready to come out. Then they peck their way out. Help them understand that the pecking is also good exercise for the new birds, so the mother will not help them with her own beak.

The children may want to play that they are baby birds in eggs. Have them scrunch up into a ball and then pretend that they are pecking their way out. You may have to show them how. (Remember to be uninhibited; children love it when their mothers act and play with them.)

If possible, let them see pictures of the eggs of different kinds of birds: a robin's blue egg, for example.

Little Chick's Story, Mary DeBall Kwitz
Meg's Eggs, Helen Nicoll
The Pinkish, Purplish, Bluish Egg, Bill Peet
Egg in the Hole Book, Richard Scarry
Egg to Chick, Millicent Selsam
How to Go About Laying an Egg, Bernard Waber
Make Way for Ducklings, Robert McCloskey

Make an "egg opener drawing," as my children call it. On a large piece of white construction paper, draw an egg. Let the children color it any way they would like. Cut it out, then cut a jagged line across the middle and attach the two halves on one side with a paper fastener. Cut a little bird out of either white or colored construction paper, and let the children color it. This is glued behind the egg, so the bird appears when the egg is "cracked" open.

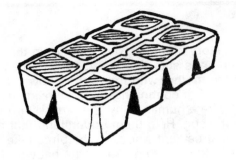

Make suet cakes to feed the birds: mix peanut butter or melted suet with bird seed and pour into egg cartons. When hardened, the whole carton can be placed outside on a window sill or other ledge for the birds.

Jelly beans make fun eggs to eat. If you have any cookie nests left from the previous day, you can put a few jelly "eggs" in these.

Deviled eggs or just hard-boiled eggs are fun, too.

DAY 4
BIRDS IN OUR AREA

Show pictures of robins, sparrows, woodpeckers, etc.—the birds that live in your part of the country. Library books are good sources here. Also, *Ranger Rick*, a magazine published by the National Wildlife Federation, is available in the children's rooms of most libraries.

Birds get their names in many ways. Some because of their color, such as the cardinal (red) and bluebird (blue). Others get their names from their cry, such as the whippoorwill. Others, from what they do: woodpeckers use their bills to peck into wood; flycatchers catch insects while they are flying. Usually, the male birds have brighter colors than the females. The female birds can hide better on their nests if their colors are not so bright.

Ask the children if they have ever seen any of these birds around. Maybe you will already have some of these birds coming to the food that you've put outside. (However, explain that sometimes it takes a week or so before birds become aware of a new feeding area.)

Sammy, the Crow Who Remembered, Elizabeth Hazelton
The Restless Robin, Marjorie Flack
The Red Horse and the Bluebird, Sandy Rabinovitz
Hi, Mr. Robin, Alvin Tresselt
Fly, Homer, Fly, Bill Peet
Sparrow Socks, George Thompson

Here is Mr. Bluebird—
Fly, Mr. Bluebird.
Here is Mr. Cardinal—
Fly, Mr. Cardinal.
Here is Mr. Oriole—
Fly, Mr. Oriole.
Here is Mr. Hummingbird—
Fly, Mr. Hummingbird.
Here is Mr. Blackbird—
Fly, Mr. Blackbird.
The birds fly and sing,
For now it is spring.

(Make a little colored bird for each color. Tape to finger when you talk about it. The children will probably want their own—this is a good way to teach colors.)

String Cheerios and popcorn and put out for the birds.

Cut out the birds that were colored in Day 1; mount on cardboard and make into a mobile.

Make a sticker game with songbird stickers.

Make popcorn: salt only what you think the children will eat and then let them put the rest out for the birds.

DAY 5
TROPICAL BIRDS

Show pictures of parrots, macaws, canaries and other tropical birds. Talk about their brightly colored plumes, and how they stand out against the dark foliage of the jungle.

Look at the beaks of these birds. Let the children guess why their beaks are so big. Talk about the kinds of food that these birds eat. Talk about the danger that they have from animals in the jungle, which might hurt them.

The Painter and Bird, Max Velthuijs
Percy the Parrot series, Wayne Carly
The Spooky Tail of Prewit Peacock, Bill Peet
But Where is the Green Parrot? Boris Zacharis
The Peacock Who Lost His Tail, John Hamberger
Tweedles be Brave! Wolo
Come Again, Pelican, Don Freeman
Nanette the Hungry Pelican, William Wise

A funny old bird is the pelican,
His bill can hold more than his belly can.

Visit a pet store or zoo and let the children see the brightly colored birds.

Make a pelican with a pocket-pouch to put fish in. Enlarge the pelican drawing shown here; draw onto cardboard and color. Cut a duplicate pattern of the pouch and cut out of heavy paper. Glue or tape the sides and the bottom to the back side of the pouch, forming a pocket. The fish can be numbered and placed in the bill in numerical order to help the children learn to count, or the fish can be different colors to help them learn colors. This can be lots of fun in many ways.

In keeping with "Polly Wants a Cracker," serve the children crackers (perhaps with jelly or cheese) as a treat.

DAY 6
HUNTING BIRDS

Show pictures of eagles, hawks and owls. Talk about how these birds are different than the little birds that we normally see around us.

Talk about how much bigger these birds are than the others we have talked about. These birds are hunting birds, since they eat small animals such as rabbits and mice. Tell the children that even though this seems cruel, it's necessary so we don't have too many of these animals, which can eat farmers' grain and do other damage.

Talk about an owl: how soft and furry its feathers look, how it sleeps during the daytime and hunts at night, how it can turn its head around on its neck to look in all directions.

The Happy Owls, Celestino Piatti
Orlando, the Brave Vulture, Tomi Ungerer
The Owl Who Hated the Dark, Earle Goodenow
Moose, Michael Foreman
Hawk, I'm Your Brother, Byrd Baylor
The Wide-Awake Owl, Louis Slobodkin
Tell Me, Mr. Owl, Doris Foster

The owl by day can't see, 'tis said!
Whoo! Whoo! Whoo!
He sits and blinks and turns his head.
Whoo! Whoo! Whoo!
But when the stars come out at night,
Whoo! Whoo! Whoo!
He calls his mate with all his might.
Whoo! Whoo! Whoo!

A wise old owl
Sat in an oak.
The more he saw,
The less he spoke.
The less he spoke,
The more he heard.
Now why can't we be
Like that wise old bird?

Make puzzles by mounting bird pictures on cardboard and cutting into pieces.

CHAPTER 9
THANKSGIVING

DAY 1
DAY 2

TURKEYS
PILGRIMS AND THANKFULNESS

Show a picture of a turkey and have the children identify it. Help them understand what makes it different from other birds—its fan-shaped tail, the way it struts around, its size, its red head, etc.

Tell them how the Indians helped the Pilgrims catch the wild turkeys that were so plentiful in the land when they arrived.

Tell them that the turkey is one of the symbols of Thanksgiving.

Turkeys, Pilgrims and Indian Corn, Edna Barth
**Sometimes It's Turkeys, Sometimes It's
     Feathers,** Lorna Balian

The following story is fun to tell, if you cut out seven colored turkeys: brown, red, blue, purple, green, yellow and white, plus single feathers in all colors but brown. If you write the verses on the backs of the turkeys, you can just about tell this without reading it. Put tacky glue or tape on the backs of the feathers, and they can be attached to the brown turkey as you go along.

Our children love this story of the turkey with a terrible temper:

Tommy was a turkey with a terrible temper. He was a little brown turkey who often flew around ranting and raging.

One day, he lost his temper over some little thing and went as red as a beet. The other little turkeys laughed and said:
"You're red, red, red as a beet,
Red from your head to the tip of your feet."

Tommy ran away and hid for a long time. When he calmed down, he realized that he was still red all over. He ran over to wise Dr. Owl to ask him what to do.

"You must learn to control that terrible temper of yours or you will be very sorry," hooted wise Dr. Owl. "That is all I can say, but come back to me in a week."

The next morning, Tommy was brown again except for a red feather in his tail.

Tommy's mother called him to come help with the Monday wash, but he got the blues as soon as he had to start working. He groaned and moaned until Mother finally told him he was acting like a baby. You can guess what happened next—he lost his temper again. This time, though, he went blue all over.

As he was running away to hide, the other turkeys yelled:
"You're blue, blue from your head to your toe: Blue all over wherever you go."

This time, Tommy blamed his mother for his losing his temper. The next morning, he was a brown little turkey again except for the blue feather next to the red one in his tail.

You can guess what happened the rest of the week. On Tuesday, Tommy didn't want to help clean up the yard. He said he hated cleaning with a purple passion. Soon, he had turned purple all over.

The turkeys all shouted:
"You're purple, purple, that's all we can see; You'd better go hide under a tree."

Of course, Tommy sat and blamed everything on everyone else. On Wednesday morning, there he was a brown turkey again, but with a purple feather along with the red one and the blue one.

He went out for a walk and saw a turkey friend eating a big ear of corn. Tommy was green with envy, because he didn't have one. Before he knew it, he was in a terrible temper tantrum and was green all over.

The turkeys turned on him and yelled:
"You're green, green, green as grass. Why don't you get wise and stop all your sass."

Tommy again went back to his hiding place and felt very sorry for himself.

The next day, he was brown, but now he had a green feather among the other brightly colored tail feathers. But something was happening to Tommy—he was beginning to really want to change. He wanted to keep his temper and decided to try harder.

Of course, all the turkeys liked to tease Tommy and in a game that they were playing, they called him a coward. Before he could think, he was having another temper tantrum and turned yellow. The turkeys were saying he had a yellow streak down his back.

They yelled:
"You're yellow, yellow just like we said.
Why don't you go home and hide under your bed."

This time, Tommy sat under the tree and thought a long time about everything. He realized that he was really the only one who could help make things better.

The next day, with his new yellow feather, he decided to really try to change. Mother asked him to watch the baby turkeys while she went shopping. When they ran through the house with muddy feet, Tommy almost lost his temper. But this time he held his breath as long as he could. It made him turn as white as a ghost, but he didn't lose his temper.

The other turkeys shouted:
"You're white, white but you're temper didn't show.
Maybe you're changing, we really hope so."

The next day, Tommy was proud to have that white feather. All day Saturday and all day Sunday, he kept calm without a single tantrum, and he was tickled pink.

On Monday, he went back to Dr. Owl and thanked him for his help. Dr. Owl told him he could wear his beautiful tail proudly now.

So, if you ever go to a farm and see a turkey with his tail all unfolded, strutting around, remember this story of the turkey with the terrible temper.

Make a target turkey picture by cutting out circles of various colors: one each—7", 6½", 4", 2½". Glue inside each other, adding a brown head. (You can use the pattern from the story on the previous page.) Add feet. This can also be fun to make the game "Pin the Head on the Turkey."

Make a mosaic turkey picture by tracing an outline of the child's hand onto a heavy piece of paper or cardboard. The inside can be filled with beans, yarn, string, buttons, seeds, cloth, etc. (This can also just be colored.)

Begin by telling the story of the Pilgrims and about how thankful they were:

Many, many years ago, a small ship came to America. It was called the *Mayflower*. The people on the ship were called Pilgrims. They wore different clothing than we do today. They had come to America to worship God as they wanted.

When they finally came to America, it was very cold and they didn't have very much food.

The Indians made friends with them and taught them how to hunt for food.

When it was spring, the weather became warm again. The Pilgrims were happy and went to work right away. They plowed the land. They planted the seeds that they had brought from England.

The sun shone all summer long. The rain watered the plants. When fall came, the Pilgrims gathered all the fruits and vegetables that they had planted. They stored them away for winter.

Everyone was happy. The Pilgrims decided to have a big feast to thank God for their food and all of their blessings. They decided to invite their Indian friends.

On the day of the feast, the Indians brought wild turkeys that they had shot with their bows and arrows. The Pilgrims covered the tables with all the good things that they had grown in their gardens.

Before anyone ate, they bowed their heads and thanked God for all their many blessings. Everyone was happy. This was the very first Thanksgiving.

Talk about all the things that the children have to be thankful for. Help them understand that on Thanksgiving Day, we shouldn't think only about all the good things to eat, but also about the many blessings that we have received during the past year.

Miranda's Pilgrims, Rosemary Well
Little Bear's Thanksgiving, Janice Brustlein
Over the River and Through the Woods, Lydia
  M. Child
The Plymouth Thanksgiving,
  Leonard Weisgard (This story is too difficult
  for the children to understand, but the
  illustrations are wonderful.)

Five little Pilgrims on Thanksgiving Day.
The 1st one said, "I'll have potatoes, if I may."
The 2nd one said, "I'll have turkey roasted."
The 3rd one said, "I'll have chestnuts toasted."
The 4th one said, "Oh, cranberries I spy,"
The 5th one said, "I'll have some pumpkin pie."

"Over the River and Through the Woods to
Grandmother's House We Go"

Make paper-bag Pilgrims to decorate the
Thanksgiving table. On a lunch bag, paint a
black belt and buttons. Stuff with newspaper.
Fold and glue top down. (This will be the
shoulders.) Add a head, a hat, arms and feet.

Children love making Pilgrim hats—they will probably want to wear them on Thanksgiving Day, too. You will need extra-large sheets of construction paper in white and black.

The boy's hat is an 11½'' circle. You can use a compass or large plate to trace this. A 6½'' circle is traced inside, but only small sections are cut out as shown. A white buckle piece can be glued onto the cone-shaped piece.

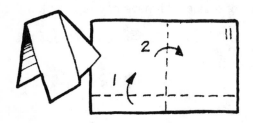

The girl's hat is a rectangle 18''x12''. Fold over one long end 4''. Then fold the whole hat in half and staple several times in the top corner.

CHAPTER 10
CHRISTMAS

DAY 1
WHAT IS CHRISTMAS?

December is a special time of year, no matter what your religious beliefs. Our family is very religious and separates Santa Claus from the birth of the Christ Child. The best friend of one of my sons is Jewish, and he celebrates Hanukkah. Whatever you prefer, this unit has plenty of ideas, which can be used for this month. We do try to spend several days celebrating Christmas traditions from other countries—they add a little extra to the fun of the season. I also think that they broaden the viewpoint of the child. Choose what works out best for you. Happy holidays!

Ask the children what special time is coming (Christmas). Tell them that this is a joyous time of year when we show our love for one another by exchanging gifts and doing nice things for other people.

Show them pictures or drawings of Christmas symbols. Help them learn what they are. Suggestions: star, wreath, candy canes, sleigh, bells, stocking, mistletoe, holly, poinsettia.

The Christmas Party, Adrienne Adams
It's Christmas, Gladys Adshead
Christmas, Dick Bruna
The Christmas Book, Dick Bruna
Nine Days to Christmas, Marie Ets
Christmas Eve, Edith Hurd
Counting the Days, James Sterling Tippett
Twelve Days of Christmas, Jack Kent

Sing "Jingle Bells." Let the children shake bells while you are singing.

Have the children make a paper chain, using alternating green and red strips of paper. Make the same number of rings as the days until Christmas. Attach to a 6" star, bell or tree cut out of colored construction paper. Hang up and let the children tear off one link each day. (This saves a lot of questions about how soon Christmas will be here!)

Make Christmas cookies.

DAY 2
CHRISTMAS TREES

Show a picture of a pine tree. Ask the children what it is. Show a picture of a Christmas tree. Ask the children what it is.

Talk about how people get their Christmas trees. Some people buy one from a Christmas tree lot in the city; some go out in the forest and cut their own tree. Others don't have a real tree at all, but use an artificial one. Some families decorate their tree early in December, and others wait until Christmas Eve.

There are many decorations for a Christmas tree. In America, we hang strings of colored lights, but in many countries, the tree is lit by little candles.

Mr. Willowby's Christmas Tree, Robert Barry
The Bird's Christmas Tree, Emma Brock
The Little Fir Tree. Margaret Brown
Christmas Tree on the Mountain, Carol Fenner
The Silver Christmas Tree, Pat Hutchins
The Biggest Christmas Tree on Earth,
     Fernando Krahn

Cut two identical trees out of green construction paper. Cut a slit up halfway in one and down halfway in the other. Join the two. These are nice grouped together in different sizes.

Cut out trees from green construction paper. Decorate with glitter and sequins. Hang from a mobile, so they can twirl and catch the light.

Decorate a tree outside for the animals. String popcorn. Dip pinecones in peanut butter and hang them on the tree with yarn. Poke orange halves onto strong branches. Hang paper cups from branches—fill with nuts or bird seed. Hang carrots down from low branches with string.

DAY 3
SANTA CLAUS

Show a picture of Santa Claus. Ask them who it is. (In our family, we don't put a lot of emphasis on Santa. We talk about him as a man who represents the spirit of giving at Christmas time. We never threaten the children to be good or Santa won't bring them any presents. Again, handle this however you want to.)

I know that there is a question in many people's minds about whether it is lying to a child to say that there is a Santa Claus. From things that we've read and from our own experience, we have decided that it is all right for the children to use their imaginations to pretend that Santa Claus, fairies and elves really live. But we talk about Santa as someone who helps parents know what children would like for Christmas, who makes the time of year more fun, etc.

Talk about the clothes that Santa wears: his cap, his red suit, his black belt, and his black boots. Ask the children what they think his big fluffy beard must feel like.

Talk about the magical reindeer who pull the sleigh, the elves who help Santa in his shop at the North Pole, the "Santa's helpers," as we call them, who help Santa talk to boys and girls in the department stores at Christmas time.

Santaberry and the Snard, Jack and Alice Schick
How Mrs. Santa Saved Christmas, Phyllis P. McGinley
Twelve Bells for Santa, Crosby Bonsall
Father Christmas, Raymond Briggs
Babar and Father Christmas, Jean de Brunhoff
Santa's Moose, Syd Hoff
Rudolph the Red-Nosed Reindeer, Robert May

Copy a large picture of Santa's face onto a piece of white paper. (A coloring book is a good source.) Let the children color it. Then have them glue cotton balls to make the beard and decorate his cap.

Make a dancing Santa. Enlarge the picture on the left. Help the children color and cut out the pieces. Attach together loosely with yarn or paper fasteners. When the children hold onto his cap and move it up and down, Santa will "dance."

DAY 4
GIFTS FOR CHRISTMAS

Show the children a wrapped gift (you can put a few pieces of candy inside). Ask them what it is (a gift or a present). Tell them that at Christmas time we give presents to others.

Ask them to think of the people in the family. Write down the names or draw a picture of each one as they mention their name. Encourage the children to make a gift for each member of their family.

Talk about the good feeling that we have inside when we give to others and don't keep thinking about what we are going to receive. You will want to re-emphasize this through the season.

Christmas is a Time for Giving, Joan Walsh Anglund
The Gift: a Portuguese Christmas Tale, Jan B. Balet
Something for Christmas, Palmer Brown
The Best Train Set Ever, Pat Hutchins
Melinda's Christmas Stocking, Ruth Jaynes
How Santa Claus had a Long and Difficult Journey Delivering his Presents, Fernando Krahn
The Night It Rained Toys, Dorothy Stephenson

Help the children make simple gifts for other members of the family. Here are a few suggestions:

Pomander: Push cloves into an orange until the whole surface is dotted. With a corsage pin, attach a long ribbon to the top so that it can be hung in a closet to freshen the air.

Bookmark: Have the child color a piece of paper the size of a bookmark. Write "Merry Christmas" and his name and date on the back. A hole can be punched in the top and a ribbon attached. Another bookmark can be made from felt. Have the child glue on circles, triangles and other designs of another color to decorate it.

Bubble Bath Jar: Have the child decorate a pretty glass canister with stickers. Fill with bubble bath.

An "Anything Can": Spray paint an empty, clean can any bright color or it can match the room of the receiver (3-lb. shortening cans are ideal). Have the child decorate it with stickers that correspond to the interest of the one who is to receive it.

DAY 5
GIFTS FOR OTHERS

Talk about other people that the children would like to give gifts to, such as grandparents and other relatives, neighbors, a Sunday School teacher. Again, write down a list of the ones to include. (Encourage them to keep this simple—you'll both get tired if the list is too long. A list of one or two is fine.)

Here are some other gift ideas for preschoolers:

Glue old Christmas cards onto the sides of a paper paint bucket. Fill with cookies or popcorn balls.

Make a pinecone candle holder: cut two pieces of corrugated cardboard into 4'' circles. Cut out a center circle so that a candle base can rest securely inside. Glue the two pieces together. Paint the outside edge or cover with a narrow strip of ribbon. Glue different-sized pinecones and nuts onto the top. Place the candle inside.

Make a candy wreath or candle holder: have the children attach pieces of wrapped peppermint or other candy to a large Styrofoam ring with small straight pins. Cover the whole wreath with candy. Include a large candle to fill the center or attach a ribbon or wire onto the back so it can be hung.

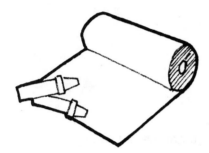

Children also enjoy decorating wrapping paper: use white shelf or freezer paper. Have the children color it with red and green markers or crayons.

DAY 6
DECORATIONS

Again talk about some of the Christmas symbols mentioned on Day 1: star, bell, holly, etc. Ask the children if they have seen any of these things this month. Perhaps they will name others as well.

Tell them that the decorations add to the excitement of Christmas. Explain that they are going to help you make some decorations for your home today.

Again, here are just a few suggestions:

Make red-and-green paper chains to decorate the tree or perhaps their bedrooms.

Roll pinecones in glue and then in glitter or sequins. Tie to tree with ribbon or yarn.

Bells: These can be made from paper nut cups or the individual sections of egg cartons. Cover with aluminum foil or colored foil paper. Poke a small hole in the top. Run a piece of ribbon through to hang. These are also pretty using several different lengths of ribbon, hanging in a group from a light fixture.

Soldier Clothespins: Using old-fashioned wooden clothespins (not the spring type), paint the top pink for the face, the main body red and the two "legs" black. Have the children help glue on a bright green pompon hat. Add facial features. Tie with ribbon to tree.

Drums: Using clean orange juice cans with lids (the kind with the plastic strip to release the lid), spray the lids and the bottom of the cans gold. Cut the sides down to three inches high. Cover with red ribbon. Gold cording can be added in a diagonal pattern. Glue top lid back on. Pin a loop of cording on the side and hang from tree.

Clothespin Reindeer: Glue two clothespins together to form legs. Glue third clothespin going up instead of down. After dry, glue on wiggly eyes, a red pompon nose and two pieces of yarn for tail. The hooves can be painted black. Tie a piece of cording around neck for hanging on tree.

We like to take several days to talk about Christmas in other lands. There are many resource books at your library with detailed information about Christmas around the world.

Here are some ideas of things you can talk about and do from a number of countries (you can decide the amount of time you want to spend):

Scandinavian countries: One morning before Christmas, our daughter, singing Christmas carols, takes a plate of Christmas rolls and a glass of hot chocolate to each family member in his/her bed. She is the Lucia Girl. We usually have a smorgasbord for dinner that night that the preschoolers help prepare that day.

Mexico: A bright piñata is part of their Christmas (see Chapter 12, Day 3 for instructions). We begin this several days in advance of our Mexican day. Then we paint and decorate it, and fill it with candy. This night we go around caroling to our neighbors and friends (our own version of the Mexican posada), and return home for enchiladas and the breaking of the piñata.

Israel: The Jewish people do not generally celebrate Christmas. Their celebration is called Hanukkah, which falls in November or December. We tell the children a simplified version of the story behind this celebration: Over 2000 years ago, the Jews rebelled against some wicked men who would not let them practice their religion. When the Jews chased them out, they found a jar of holy oil which would burn one day. By a miracle, it burned for eight. A candle is lit each night for eight nights—a special holder used to hold the candles is called the menorah. Latkes or potato pancakes can be served. If you can find a "dreidel," which is a Hanukkah toy top, at a synagogue or temple gift shop, it would be fun for the children to learn to play with it.

Plum Pudding for Christmas, Virginia Kahl
Baboushka and the Three Kings, Ruth Robbins
Twelve Days of Christmas, illustrated by Susan Swan
An Edwardian Christmas, John S. Goodall
9 Days to Christmas, Marie H. Ets
The Christmas Piñata, Jack Kent
Din Dan Don, It's Christmas, Janina Domanska
Christmas in the Stable, Astrid Lindgren
The Power of Light (8 Stories for Hanukkah), Isaac Singer
Noël for Jeanne-Marie, Françoise Seignolose

Other days can be spent making Christmas cookies, breads or other holiday foods. Just remember to keep the whole month simple and don't wear yourself out! There is so much excitement in the air that the children don't need a lot to keep them pretty keyed up.

CHAPTER 11
WINTER

DAY 1
WHAT IS WINTER?

Talk about what happens in the winter. What does the world look like? (If you live in an area that doesn't have snow or the traditional things of winter, talk about how your climate changes.) You might want to discuss the many things about winter that we'll be talking about later on in this unit.

Talk about where the leaves have gone. How have the grass changed color and plants died down?

Talk about how icicles are made of frozen water. Try to show them one or let them feel an ice cube. Talk about what it feels like, what it tastes like; examine the little bubbles that form inside.

Take a glass, fill it with ice and in about an hour (when the outside is frozen and the inside isn't), you can see an air bubble, or you can shake it and still hear water. Make a small hole in the top toward one side. Run hot water over the outside, just until the ice is released from the glass. Drain any water left inside. The resulting "cube" is fun to look at, and the kids will love to eat it.

A Day of Winter, Betty Miles
A Pocketful of Seasons, Doris Foster
I Like Winter, Lois Lenski
Winter is Here, Jane B. Moncure
The Snowy Day, Ezra J. Keats
The Big Snow, Berta and Elmer Hader
All Ready for Winter, Leone Adelson
Winter's Coming, Eve Bunting
Stopping by Woods on a Snowy Evening,
   Robert Frost. Illustrated by Susan Jeffers
   (Her pictures are just beautiful!)

Sing a song of winter, frost is in the air.
Sing a song of winter, snowflakes everywhere,
Sing a song of winter, hear the sleigh bells chime.
Can you think of anything as nice as wintertime?
(*to the tune of "Sing a Song of Sixpence"*)

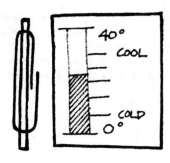

Make little thermometers out of paper. Mark degrees between 40 and 0 (or whatever best approximates your temperatures at this time). Cut a slit at the top and bottom. Cut one red and one white piece of ribbon; glue one end of each together. Insert through slits in paper and glue other ends together on back. The temperature can then be made to go up and down as the temperature does outside. (You may want to save this to use in spring when the temperature begins to rise.) Or just mark freezing, colder, cold, chilly, or whatever, up the side.

Freeze juice in ice cube trays. Insert a toothpick as a handle. Or freeze Maraschino cherries, banana slices or other fuits that take freezing well, in ice cube trays; cover with water and freeze. Have them later in clear soda pop as a treat.

Besides the ice treats mentioned above, Popsicles are also fun for children.

DAY 2
WHAT DO ANIMALS DO IN THE WINTER?

Tell the children that when it's cold, people put on warm clothes. The animals do different things to protect themselves. Many birds fly south, where the weather is warmer. Some animals hibernate. When the world becomes colder, their bodies tell them to go to sleep. Mammals, such as bears, eat lots of food all summer long, and then sleep all winter. Others, such as mice and rabbits, store lots of food in their dens with them. There, they can eat and stay warm until spring comes.

Show pictures of animals whose colorings change in the winter: the fur on rabbits changes from brown to white; the coloring on many birds becomes duller or even white in the winter to blend in with their surroundings.

Buzzy Bear's Winter Party, Dorothy Marino
When Winter Comes, Russell Freedman

Make little matching cards for the children to match the animal with where it lives in the winter: butterfly—cocoon; bear—cave; rabbit—hole in the ground; beaver—home in streams.

Take a walk in a woods or other natural area. Try to spot the tracks of animals in the snow. Try to decide what they belong to.

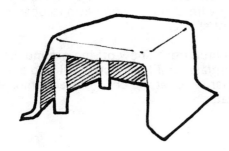

Make a bear "cave" by covering a card table with blankets. This is a fun place to eat lunch, too.

Talk about where snow comes from. Snow comes from clouds, just as rain does. When it is very cold, the water freezes to form snow crystals, which we call snowflakes. If many snow crystals cling together, the snowflakes may be very large.

Talk about snowflakes. All flakes have six sides or six points, but no two are alike.

Allow some flakes to drop onto a dark blue or black piece of construction paper. Quickly look at them with a magnifying glass to observe the different shapes.

Skim a little fresh snow off the ground. Let the children taste it. Place a cup of it into a saucepan, and let the children see it melt back into water.

The Snowy Day, Ezra J. Keats
Snow, John Burningham
Snowtime, Miriam Schlein
White Snow, Bright Snow, Alvin Tresselt

Cut snowflakes from folded paper. Tape to the windows or hang from a mobile.

Make dough snowflakes, mixing 1 c. salt, 2 c. flour, and 1 c. water. (Add more or less water so dough is not too sticky.) Knead 7-10 minutes. Roll dough about ¼"-½" thick. Cut into a basic shape with a large cookie cutter. The small details can be cut out with small hors d'oeuvres cutters or a knife (with Mommy's help). Bake at 325 degrees until golden, about 20-30 minutes. These can then be varnished or spread with glue and sprinkled with glitter. Then hang them with yarn or string in a window.

Make pasta snowflakes: lay out different shapes of pasta onto a piece of waxed paper and glue together. Use wagon wheels, corkscrews, bow ties and other shapes. The finished flakes can be sprayed gold or silver and hung.

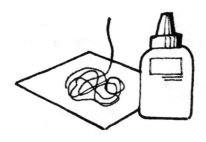

Form string snowflakes by dipping string in glue and then forming into shapes on waxed paper. These can be hung when dry, too.

Shave or crush ice into glasses, put fruit juice or punch over and make snow cones.

Make snow cream: fill a bowl with fresh, clean snow and pour real maple syrup over and mix. Also good with syrup heated just until boiling and poured over.

DAY 4
WHAT DO WE DO IN THE WINTER?

Show clothes from magazines or catalogs. Ask which we wear for winter. Why?

Pretend we are going outdoors. Let the children pantomime what they would put on.

Have them pretend that they are skating outside, putting on the skates first. Then skiing, sledding, etc.

Let the children practice zipping their coats to prepare to go outside and hooking their own boots (depending on their age).

The Mitten, Alvin Tresselt
Katy and the Big Snow, Virginia Burton
The Bears' Christmas, Stan and Jan
  Berenstain
Snow Fun, Caroline Levine

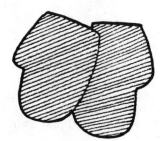

Cut red mittens from cardboard to hang up. Add this verse:
"Thumbs in the thumb place, Fingers all together,
This is the song we sing in winter weather."

Make a snowing paperweight: thoroughly wash an empty baby-food jar, removing the label. Glue a small plastic house, person or animal to inside of lid, let dry. Put 2 T. moth flakes into jar and fill with water, adding a drop of blue food coloring if desired. Replace lid to make sure that there is enough water to fill the jar but not overflow. Dry lid and top of jar. Glue threads of lid and screw on tightly. (Remember that moth flakes are poisonous, so be careful when using them around the children.)

Make "snowballs" (popcorn balls) to eat.

DAY 5
SNOWMEN

Using cutout white paper circles, build a snowman on blue paper, talking about the different parts. Take the pieces apart and let the child build the snowman.

Pretend you are building a snowman. Have one of the children pretend to be the snowman. Ask "What will happen to the snowman?" Have the children pretend to be melting snowmen.

On a cookie sheet or in a pan, form three balls out of snow. Add eyes, nose and other features. Watch what happens to it as it gets warm inside.

The Self-Made Snowman, Fernando Krahn
Dear Snowman, Janosh
The Snowman, Raymond Briggs

A chubby little snowman had a carrot nose.
(Form snowman with fist.)
Along came a bunny and what do you suppose? *(Hold up two fingers of other hand; hop around.)*
That hungry little bunny, looking for his lunch,
Ate that snowman's carrot nose—*(Pretend to bite a carrot.)*
Crunch, crunch, crunch. *(Pretend to chew.)*

Make snowmen from buttons glued onto paper. Add yarn for scarf and draw on hat.

Glue cotton balls onto colored paper to make snowmen.

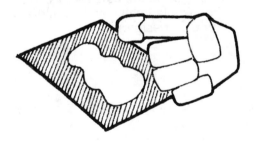

Draw a snowman picture: beat up Ivory Snow with a little water until the consistency of fingerpaint. Let the children draw a picture with it on blue or black construction paper.

Make a paper snowman by rolling 2"-wide strips of white paper into circles, making three sizes. Add a hat, facial features and arms with black construction paper.

Make snowmen treats by attaching large marshmallows together with toothpicks, adding raisin features with Karo syrup "glue."

Make an ice cream snowman: use a large scoop of vanilla ice cream for the body and a marshmallow for the head. Use cloves for the features. A chocolate cookie with a large gumdrop on top can be the hat. These can be made up for the whole family by the children. (Or devise your own design.)

DAY 6
SNOWPLAY

This day is spent in play in the snow—Mom and the children. Here are a couple of fun ideas to try:

Take large empty milk cartons. Pack tightly with snow. Remove the blocks to make a snow fort.

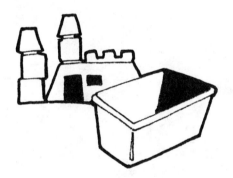

Make a snow castle using bread pans packed with snow.

Make giant footprints out of heavy cardboard. Center a child's foot on each and make a hole in the cardboard on each side of his/her foot. Thread heavy string or twine through the holes, tie onto boots and make monster tracks.

CHAPTER 12
TRANSPORTATION

Show pictures of different kinds of cars. Talk about what makes them different—body shapes, number of people they will hold, for example. (Just talk about the outside—children will not understand what's under the hood—I don't really!)

Show pictures of old-fashioned cars. Talk about how cars have changed—shape, tires, how they start, features like windshield wipers, lights, etc.

Talk about the different parts of a car—wheels, lights, doors, steering wheel, horn, trunk, engine, window. This is a good time to explain to them never to play in cars or to play with the parts of a car.

I think it's a good idea to keep your car locked when it's parked in your driveway so that children are not tempted to play in it.

Talk about how we act around cars. We should look both ways before crossing streets. We shouldn't play in the street or ride Big Wheels or tricycles in the street. We should always wear a seat belt or sit in a car seat (for young children). We keep our arms and heads inside the car and keep the doors locked while the car is moving.

(As a mother, make sure you set a good example and be firm and consistent in expecting the children to obey these safety rules.)

ABC of Cars and Trucks, Anne Alexander
Little Old Automobile, Marie Ets
The Little Auto, Lois Lenski
Jennifer and Josephine, Bill Peet
Cars and Trucks and Things That Go, Richard Scarry
The Great Big Car and Truck Book, Richard Scarry
If I Drove a Car, Miriam Young
The Giant Nursery Book of Things That Go, George J. Zaffo

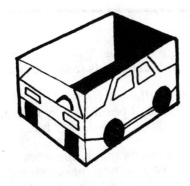

Get a big box the child can sit down in (the size that cartons of eggs are delivered to the grocery store in is perfect). Paint the sides or cover with butcher paper. Decorate so that it will look like a car. Let the child pretend that he is driving around in his car. (Save the box for Day 2, Buses.)

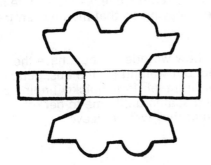

Make a paper car. Enlarge this pattern, let children color. Fold and tape.

Make a race-car hot dog (see Food, Chapter 6, Day 4).

Make a cookie car: cut out pieces of rolled dough for the body, wheels, lights and other parts. Press smaller pieces onto the body. Bake.

Show a picture of a bus. Talk about how it is different from a car (holds many people).

Talk about the different kinds of buses, showing pictures, if possible: city bus, school bus, touring bus, double-decker bus.

Talk about the things that a bus driver does: takes the people's money, makes sure everyone gets on and off the bus safely, makes sure everyone stays seated, checks the engine and lights before leaving so that the bus can travel safely.

Talk about how we ride the bus: have the children act out waiting for the bus, getting on the bus, paying their fare, quickly finding a seat, staying seated until time to get off, signaling that they want to leave.

Bus Ride, Nancy Jewell
ABC of Buses, Dorothy Shuttlesworth
If I Drove a Bus, Miriam Young
General transportation books listed on
   Day 1

Take a ride in a bus. Help the children remember the things that they have practiced.

Make a bus picture. Let the children draw the people behind the windows.

Using the box from Day 1, remove the butcher paper and make the box into a bus.

DAY 3
TRUCKS

Show pictures of trucks—talk about all the different kinds of trucks.

Talk about what makes a truck different from a car—usually heavier; used for different jobs. rather than carrying people; generally bigger tires to go over rougher ground; etc.

Help the children learn to identify several frequently seen trucks: delivery truck, dump truck, pickup truck, garbage truck, cement truck, semi-trailer.

Mike Mulligan and His Steam Shovel, Virginia
    Burton
The Truck on the Track, Janet Burroway
Truck Drivers: What Do They Do? Carla
    Greene
If I Drove a Truck, Miriam Young
The Big Book of Real Trucks, George J. Zaffo
Let's Go Trucks, David L. Harrison
General transportation books listed on
    Day 1.

Visit a construction site. Let the children watch the trucks and talk about the job that each truck has.

From an empty milk carton, make a semi-trailer. Cover the carton with paper. Draw on features. This can also be used in different sizes to make other kinds of trucks.

DAY 4
TRAINS

Show a picture of an old train. Talk about the parts—smoke stack, wheels, bell, light, engineer's seat, wood or coal bin, engine.

Show a picture of a modern train. Talk about the new parts—whistle instead of bell, more wheels, diesel engines that burn fuel oil like cars instead of coal. Explain that modern trains travel much more quickly than the old ones.

Show pictures of the different cars on a train, such as coal car, cattle car, flat car, oil car, caboose. Help the children learn the names. (If you have problems identifying these, most train books listed below will be helpful in explaining the parts of a train and what they do.)

Freight Train, Donald Crews
The Little Train, Graham Greene
The Little Engine That Could, Watty Piper
The Caboose Who Got Loose, Bill Peet
The Little Train, Lois Lenski
If I Drove a Train, Miriam Young
The Everyday Train, Amy Ehrlich
Two Little Trains, Margaret Brown
Little Red Caboose, Marian Potter
The Big Book of Real Trains, Elizabeth
   Cameron
Hop Aboard! Here We Go! Richard Scarry
General transportation books listed on
   Day 1

"I've Been Working on the Railroad"

"Down by the Station"

Down by the station
Early in the morning
See the little puffer-bellies
All in a row.
See the station master
Pull the little whistle.
Puff, puff, toot, toot,
Off we go.

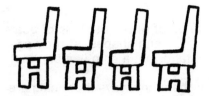

Make a "train" from chairs. Let the children pretend to be different workers on a train—engineer, conductor, porter.

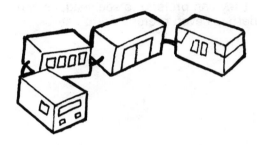

Make a box train using small boxes attached together with yarn. They can be decorated as different train cars.

Show pictures of different kinds of boats. Talk about the sizes and shapes. At their age, they can understand that a ship is a big boat.

Talk about the many ways that boats are powered: muscle power—canoes, kayaks, rowboats; wind—sailboats, schooners; motors—speedboats, ships, ocean liners; fuel and paddle—paddle-wheelers.

Have the children pretend that they are on board a boat. They can rock gently back and forth. They can pretend to see seagulls and fish, perhaps even pretending to fish.

Little Toot series, Hardie Gramatky
The Little Sail Boat, Lois Lenski
Burt Dow Deep-Water Man, Robert McCloskey
The Boats on the River, Marjorie Flack
Tim series, Edward Ardizzone
If I Sailed a Boat, Miriam Young
Henry the Castaway, Mark Taylor
The Little Sailboat, Lois Lenski
The Big Book of Real Boats and Ships,
   George Zaffo
Great Steamboat Mystery, Richard Scarry

"Row, Row, Row Your Boat"

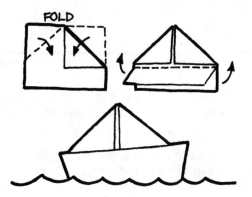

Make paper boats—float them in the bathtub or a nearby stream.

Make boats from empty plastic containers such as margarine or nondairy whipping cream. Punch holes on the sides, at the top edge, and tie together to make a whole fleet for your bathtub.

Make egg boats: prepare stuffed hard-boiled egg halves. Make a sail from a slice of cheese threaded with a toothpick. Olives can be the passengers.

Show pictures of different kinds of airplanes. Let them see old-fashioned planes as well as modern jets.

Talk about the parts of a plane: wings, cockpit (where the pilot sits), tail, propellers or jet engines.

Talk about helicopters and how they are different from airplanes: propellers on top; can go up and down rather than taking off on a runway. (Again, if you have problems identifying these, check in the books listed below.)

Loopy, Hardie Gramatky
The Little Airplane, Lois Lenski
We Fly, Alfred Olschewski
Richard Scarry's Great Big Air Book, Richard Scarry
If I Flew a Plane, Miriam Young
The Big Book of Real Airplanes, George J. Zaffo
General transportation books mentioned on Day 1

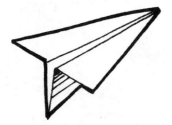

Make paper airplanes to fly. Here's an example in case you, like me, never made a paper airplane until you became a mother.

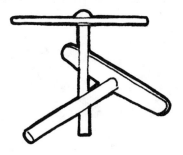

Make tongue-depressor helicopters: a thumb tack or small nail through the center of a tongue depressor. Attach to the eraser end of a pencil or small dowel. When the stick is rubbed between the palms of your hands with the depressor on top, the "helicopter" will take off.

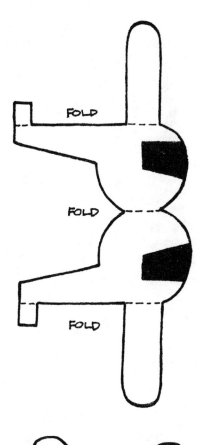

FOLD

FOLD

FOLD

Make a paper helicopter: using this picture as a pattern, draw the helicopter onto a heavy piece of paper, folding as shown on the dotted lines. Glue or tape the two sides of the helicopter together. This is fun to hold up high; or, stand at the top of the stairs and let it twirl down.

CHAPTER 13
HELPERS IN THE COMMUNITY

DAY 1
MAILMAN

Bring some letters and ask how they got to your home.

Watch for your mail carrier and have the children say "hi" to him/her. Have the children ask him what he does on his job.

Arrange to have them receive a letter from the mailman that you have sent them ahead of time.

Act out being a mailman, sorting letters into different boxes at the post office, placing them in their mailbag, walking down the street to deliver them.

Country Mailman, Jerrold Beim
The Post Office Book, Gail Gibbons
  (an excellent book)
First Class! Harold Roth

Make mailman hats: cut lunch bags down to a 5" height, with the front cut in a semicircle for the brim.

Talk about the equipment that a mailman needs to deliver the mail: trucks to get around in, bags to carry all the letters, mailboxes to put the mail into.

Walk down the block and look at all the different mailboxes that people have. Have the children notice that the houses have numbers on them so that the mailman knows where to deliver the mail.

Make little mailbags out of grocery bags. Tie string through the top to fit over the child's shoulder. They can color their bags or place stickers on them to resemble stamps.

Show several letters to the children. Ask them how the mail carrier knew that they belonged to your family. Point out the address.

On a large piece of paper, draw a pretend envelope. Talk about the return address, the address and the stamp.

Let the children write a letter to someone special: a relative or friend. Let them lick the stamp for the envelope (Be sure to emphasize that stamps are only for licking if Mother says that they may—if not, you may find your stamps all carefully stuck to the wall, as I once did!)

Let them write or draw little letters to other family members. Give them fake stamps (stickers, Christmas seals) to put on them. Let the children put them in their mailbag and deliver one to the dresser or room of each member of the family.

A Letter to Amy, Ezra Keats
Adventures of a Letter, G. Warren Schloat
Linda's Air Mail Letter, Norman Bell
On Beyond Zebra, Theodor Seuss Geisel

Take the letters that they have written to a relative or friend to the post office to mail. Perhaps you can go for a little tour, so that the children can see what will happen to their letters.

DAY 4
FIREMEN

Show the children a good book with pictures of firemen in action and talk about what they do.

Show a play fire truck. Talk about the different parts; such as the ladder, the hose, the siren. What do you think they are used for?

Show pictures of what firemen wear. Have the children pretend that they are putting on the heavy pants, boots, coat and hat.

Visit your neighborhood fire hydrant. Talk about what it is called and how the fire fighters use it.

Use this time to talk to the children about the dangers of fire and matches. Please help them to understand fully that matches are for adults, not children. Tell them not to stand too close to a fire in the fireplace because little sparks could fly out and burn them. Also, if you have a kerosene heater in the winter time, make sure that they understand it can burn them. Fire stations frequently have illustrated booklets that can teach children about fire and safety, too.

The Big Book of Real Fire Engines, Elizabeth Cameron
Big Book of Real Fire Engines, George J. Zaffo
Blue Bug's Safety Book, Virginia Poulet
The Little Fire Engine, Lois Lenski
I Want to be a Fireman, Graham Greene
Jim Fireman, Roger Bester
Fireman Brown, Harry Bernstein
Fireman Save My Cat! Tony Palazzo

Down the street the engine goes;
The firemen chase the fire.
Up the ladder with their hose—
Out goes the fire.

(sung to the tune of "Pop Goes the Weasel")

From red construction paper, cut out a fire hat, following the directions in Chapter 10, Day 2, Pilgrim Hats. Cut out center section as illustrated.

Wearing their fire hats, raincoats and boots, the children can play fireman. Perhaps you have a small old piece of hose that they can also use.

Of course, this is the right day to visit the fire station. We have found the firemen to be more than helpful, even if you are taking just one or two children on a tour.

DAY 5
POLICEMEN

Talk about the many things that police officers do: help people drive their cars correctly, help children cross the street, help children get home when they are lost. (Emphasize the good!)

Have the children pretend that they are lost and you are the police officer. Ask them questions like: "What is your name?" "What is your daddy's name?" "Where do you live?" "What is your phone number?" (Although they may be a little young for this, they need to learn this information as soon as possible.)

Try to get a book from the library with pictures of what the police do. Don't read the words to the children as much as talk to them about what is going on in the pictures.

Make arrangements to visit a police station. Our oldest son had a marvelous time at the age of four on this visit. One policeman even let him push the siren for a few seconds on his car in the parking lot. This is an important time for the children to learn that the police are their friends. (Please do not use police officers as "meanies" who are going to come and put them in jail when they are naughty. The police are really to help and protect us, and children will do so much better in their relationships with them if this is emphasized.)

Make Way for Ducklings, Robert McCloskey (A family of ducks is befriended by a kind policeman.)
Policeman Small, Lois Lenski
On the Beat—Policeman at Work, Barry Robinson and Martin Dain
I Want to be a Police Officer, Donna Baker
Safety Can Be Fun, Munro Leaf
Green Says, "Go," Ed Emberly
Red Light, Green Light, Golden MacDonald

Twinkle, twinkle, traffic light,
Shining on the corner bright.
When it's green, it's time to go.
When it's red, it's stop you know.
Twinkle, twinkle, traffic light,
Shining on the corner bright.

(to the tune of "Twinkle, Twinkle, Little Star"—fun to act out, too)

Visit a police station.

Take a walk through your neighborhood, following the signs and looking both directions when you cross the streets.

DAY 6
OTHER WORKERS

Have the children think of other people who help us. Ask: "When Daddy's suits are dirty, where does he take them?" (cleaners) "When I need some food, where do I go?" (grocer) Continue on with the butcher, barber, hardware store man, druggist, gas station attendant, garbage man and others.

Have them pretend that they are going into a store and need some help. Help them learn to speak to other people with confidence.

Wake Up, City, Alvin Tresselt
City Poems, Lois Lenski
At Work, Richard Scarry
Jobs People Do, Jane Moncure
Busiest People Ever, Richard Scarry
What Do People Do All Day? Richard Scarry

On a large piece of pellon interfacing, you can draw a little city with markers. Include buildings for the different helpers that you have talked about this week, homes, stop signs on the corners, etc. The children can then drive little cars or walk with their fingers through the town and visit the helpers.

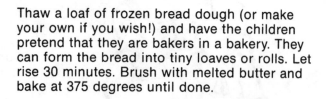

Thaw a loaf of frozen bread dough (or make your own if you wish!) and have the children pretend that they are bakers in a bakery. They can form the bread into tiny loaves or rolls. Let rise 30 minutes. Brush with melted butter and bake at 375 degrees until done.

You might want to take the children on a field trip to visit a drugstore, a barbershop, a gas station. Ask the owner to explain to the children what he/she does.

CHAPTER 14
HEALTH

DAY 1
TAKING CARE OF OUR BODIES

Show a bar of soap and ask what it is used for. Ask, "How does it smell?" (You might want to have several kinds to smell.) Place it in some water and rub your hands back and forth to make bubbles. Talk about how the bubbles carry the dirt and bad germs away. Show the children how to wash their hands properly. Let the children try it in either a dishpan or a sink.

Make a puppet for your hand by putting a facial tissue over your fist and putting a rubber band around your wrist. A face can then be drawn on the tissue. Let this puppet talk about how we take care of sneezes and runny noses, using a tissue to catch the germs.

Talk about the importance of taking baths, washing your hair, and changing into clean underwear and clothes every day.

Let them brush your hair, and talk about how brushing will help their hair not only look nice, but also be pretty and shiny. Let them brush each other's hair. Make sure that they are careful and don't pull or snarl each other's hair.

Talk about how important it is for our bodies to get good food and enough sleep. Tell them a story about a little car and how it ran out of gas because it had been driven too long. Then, it overheated because it hadn't had a rest. Our bodies need "fuel" to help them keep going, too.

Minnie the Mump, Paul Tripp
**Phoebe Dexter has Harriet Peterson's
   Sniffles,** Laura Numeroff

Make soap bubbles that the children can blow with either a straw or a small funnel. (You can just mix some dishwashing liquid in water, but I don't think the bubbles hold together as well.)

2 c. warm water
6 T. glycerine
6 T. dishwashing liquid
dash sugar

Mix well. Let stand about a half hour before using.

Make fingerpaint by mixing Ivory Snow (or any soap flakes) with enough water to make thick paste. Whip until it is the consistency of heavy cream. Food coloring can be added. Paint on the shiny side of freezer paper (it's less expensive than fingerpaint paper) or let the children paint the inside of the bathtub. When they are through, just turn on the water and give them a bubble bath!

Give each child his own package of Kleenex, soap and hand lotion. (You can often buy samples at the drugstore that are good for this.)

DAY 2
DENTISTS AND TEETH

Ask the children who helps them keep their teeth clean. What does he do? If you have a younger child who has not yet seen the dentist, take the time to explain more.

Pretend you are a dentist, and look at their teeth. Count how many teeth they have and tell them how nice and white they look.

Put a large drawing of a tooth on the board or wall. Put brown spots of paper on it to show food and sugar. Use a large brush to remove them—I use the snow brush from the car. Tape the brown spots on very lightly, so they can easily be removed by the brush.

Have the children brush their teeth. Then have them chew red disclosing tablets (available from your dentist or a drugstore). Let the children see the places where they need to brush better—where their teeth have red left on them from the tablets. Then have them brush again, paying particular attention to those areas.

My dentist has said that parents should brush their children's teeth until they are in school. Sometimes the children object, so this example of the red disclosing tablets helps them see why they need parents' help. While I brush their teeth, however, I explain to them what I am doing—brushing carefully away from the gums, getting all the way to the back, brushing all the surfaces. When I floss their teeth (which should be done once a day), I also explain to them what I am doing and why.

The Mango Tooth, Charlotte Pomerantz
Albert's Toothache, Barbara Williams
A Visit to the Dentist, Mary Packard
My Dentist, Anne Rockwell
Little Rabbit's Loose Tooth, Lucy Bates
Alligator's Toothache, Diane de Groat

I have a little toothbrush. *(Pretend to hold out a toothbrush.)*
I hold it very tight. *(Pretend to hold tight.)*
I brush my teeth each morning *(Pretend to brush teeth.)*
And again at night.

Make teeth out of playdough.

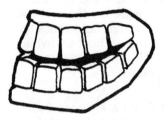

Give each child a new toothbrush.

Serve a treat made with a milk product. Explain that milk is very good for our teeth because it contains calcium, which helps make teeth and bones strong.

Ask the children who helps them get better when they are sick. Talk about their doctor and about what a nice man/woman he/she is.

Bring a play doctor's kit: talk about what the different instruments are for—stethoscope, thermometer, otoscope (to look in ears), tongue depressor, reflex hammer.

Have them talk about the reasons that they go to visit the doctor's office. Help them feel comfortable with the experiences that they have had. Help them understand that although doctors sometimes have to hurt us (when they give shots, for example), they love us and want us to feel well and happy.

Nicky Goes to the Doctor, Richard Scarry
Curious George Goes to the Hospital,
    H.R. Rey
Doctors and Nurses, Graham Greene
Muffy in the Hospital, Dick Bruna
Madeline, Ludwig Bemelmans
Jeff's Hospital Book, Harriet Sobol
Betsy and the Doctor, Gunilla Wolde

Miss Polly had a dolly, who was sick, sick, sick.
So, she called for the doctor to come quick, quick, quick.
The doctor came with his bag and his hat,
And he knocked on the door with a rat-a-tat-tat.
He looked at the dolly and he shook his head.
He said, "Miss Polly, put her straight to bed."
He wrote on the paper for a pill, pill, pill.
"I'll be back in the morning with my bill, bill, bill."

(Children love acting this out.)

Five little monkeys jumping on the bed.*(Five fingers from one hand jump on the other palm.)*
One fell off and broke his head. *(Hold head with hands.)*
Momma called the doctor *(Pretend to dial and hold a receiver.)*
And the doctor said,
"There'll be no more monkeys, jumping on the bed." *(Shake finger in anger.)*

(Repeat, eliminating a monkey each time on down to "No more monkeys jumping on the bed.")

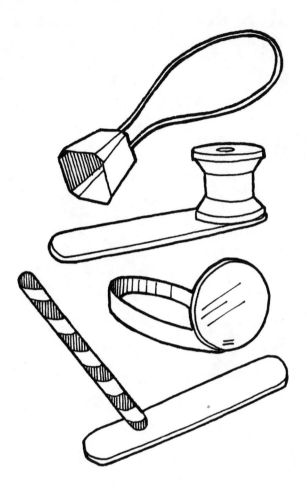

Help the children make their own doctor's kits:

Stethoscope: one compartment from an egg carton strung with yarn or string.
Otoscope: empty spool of thread glued to a tongue depressor.
Mirror: circle of cardboard covered with foil and stapled to a paper headband.
Thermometer: a candy stick
Tongue depressor

As you serve apple treats, tell the children the old saying: "An apple a day keeps the doctor away." (You might want to mention that this is only a saying, and an orange a day is just as good.)

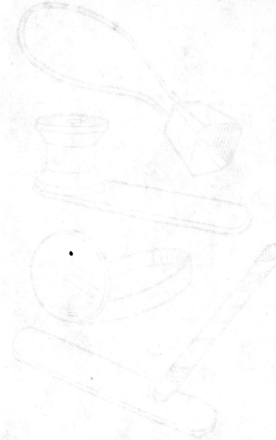

CHAPTER 15
VALENTINE'S DAY

DAY 1
WHAT IS VALENTINE'S DAY?

Hold up a red paper heart. What is this? (heart) Now put a doily behind it. Now what is this? (Valentine)

Talk about how Valentine's Day is one special day during the year when we let people we love know how much we care for and appreciate them.

Show a picture of Cupid. Say, "We sometimes see this boy's picture around Valentine's Day. His name is Cupid. He supposedly shoots arrows at people to make them love each other. He helps us to remember to make other people happy. How can we make others happy?"

Our Valentine Book, Jane Moncure
Valentine's Day, Joyce Kessel

Color with white chalk on bright-red construction-paper hearts.

Let the children string small precut paper hearts on yarn with a needle. These can be separated with 1" pieces of soda straw. The yarn can be made into a necklace or used to decorate the room.

Again with white yarn and a large needle, let the children sew back and forth through red material or felt hearts to make a design.

Make a heart tree: cut out hearts from different sizes of red paper. Tape or tie a piece of string to each heart. Tie the hearts to a small, dead tree branch. Support the branch in a jar or can filled with small pebbles or marbles.

Again, talk about why we have valentines. Have them think of someone special to give a valentine to, for example, a lonely neighbor, or a special person that they come in contact with. (Remember that small children are usually very happy to give only one or two valentines.)

She Loves Me, She Loves Me Not, Robert Keeshan
Little Love Story, Fernando Krahn
Bee My Valentine, Miriam Cohen
Pleasant Fieldmouse's Valentine Trick, Jan Wahl

Sign and address either homemade or store-bought valentines for the friends and family discussed above.

Make valentine animals: use different-sized hearts. The ideas are endless, but here are a few.

Make and frost valentine cookies for the family.

DAY 3
LET'S HAVE A VALENTINE PARTY

Children enjoy simple games at their parties. You may want to invite several of their friends to participate with you this day.

Games:

Heart Relay Race: Cut out hearts for as many actions as your children have mastered: hop, skip, run, jump, walk backwards, somersault. If you have enough children, make two sets and they can race. With just one or two, have them just pick a heart; you read them the word and have them do it down to the end of the room and back. They also think it's fun if Mommy does this, too!

Hide tiny hearts around the room and let them try to find them.

Have them take turns thinking of as many things as they can that are red.

Make cupcakes and frost with pink or red frosting.

Serve any flavor red Jello (strawberry, cherry, etc.).

Make frosted pretzels (they look like little hearts):
1 can vanilla frosting with red food coloring added, or your favorite frosting
1 package pretzels

Melt frosting in top of double boiler until liquid. Remove from heat but leave frosting over hot water. Dip pretzels into frosting, then place on waxed paper. Let dry 8 hours. This could be a fun activity to make for the party and then serve to the rest of the family at dinner.

CHAPTER 16
THE OCEAN

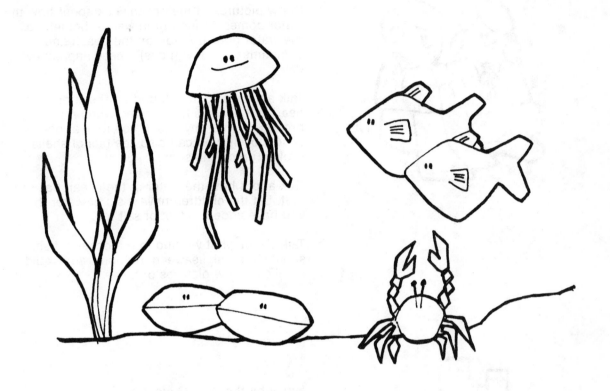

DAY 1
WHAT IS THE OCEAN?

Show pictures of the ocean. Talk about how the water comes in and out in waves. Sometimes the water goes up high on the beach and sometimes it is low (tides). These happen every day.

Talk about sand. It is found on the shores of nearly all oceans. It is formed when rocks are broken up into tiny bits. If you look at ocean sand closely, you can also see bits of shells broken up on the shore.

Talk about how the water in the ocean has salt in it. Let the children have a sip of water that you have added ½ tsp. of salt to.

Talk about what we find in the oceans: fish, shellfish, coral, seaweed, octopus, and squid families. Show pictures of these.

Harry by the Sea, Gene Zion
Blue Bug's Beach Party, Virginia Poulet
The Bears' Nature Guide, Stan and Jan
    Berenstain, pp. 38-39
Under the Ocean, Eugene Booth (a marvelous
    thinking book)
A Day at the Beach, Mircea Vasiliu

If you live near the ocean, plan a visit for the day and let the children see many of the things you have talked about.

Grow your own "coral": place several pieces of broken brick or soft coal the size of large walnuts in a small aluminum pie pan or saucer. Then mix together:

4 T. non-iodized salt
4 T. liquid bluing
4 T. water
1 T. household ammonia

Pour slowly over pieces in dish. Then carefully drop small amounts of food coloring over the rocks. In just a short time, little crystals will begin to form. Don't move it around too much or touch it, because your "coral" will crumble easily.

Make or buy saltwater taffy as a treat this day.

Show pictures of fish. Talk about the different parts of a fish and what they are used for: the tail helps the fish move through the water; fins help the fish change directions; and eyes without eyelids let fish see underwater more easily.

Explain that fish do not breathe air, as we do. They have gills on both sides of their bodies, which take the air out of the water for them.

If you can get a good book on fish from your library, you can show the children the different features of fish that protect them from their enemies: certain colors or the ability to change colors, false or giant eye marks to confuse other fish, etc.

Explain that some fish live in salt water and some in freshwater. Talk about each.

Burt Dow, Deep-Water Man, Robert McCloskey
Fish Out of School, Evelyn Shaw
The Little Black Fish, Sammed Bahrang
The Little Spotted Fish, Jane Yolen
Swimmy, Leo Lionni
Fish is Fish, Leo Lionni
Goldfish, Herbert Zim

Let the children "go fishing." Cut out different fish shapes 2" long, from cardboard. Have the children color them. Attach pieces of magnetic strips. (These can be purchased at office supply, hobby or fabric stores.) Tie a paper clip onto a piece of string, and attach to a dowel or stick. (It's easier for younger children to just use the string.)

Make a mosaic fish picture: cut a large fish picture out of heavy cardboard. Apply white glue to cardboard a little area at a time and let the children add corn, split peas, navy beans and rice to fish to make designs.

Visit an aquarium or fish store to look at the fish.

Make tuna fish sandwiches.

DAY 3
SHELLS AND SHELLFISH

Show pictures of shells or have some for the children to hold. Tell them that these used to be houses for animals that live in the ocean. They make their shells out of minerals from the water. As the animals grow, so do their shells. When they die, the shell is left behind.

Let them feel the hard outsides of shells and the smooth, shiny insides.

Show them a pearl (an artificial one is fine!). Explain that this is from an oyster. A little grain of sand got into the shell. To protect himself, the oyster covered the sand with secretions. The grain of sand became a pearl. Men dive deep down into the ocean to bring up oysters, hoping to find valuable pearls inside.

Herman, the Helper, Robert Krauss
I Saw the Sea Come In, Alvin Tresselt
Kermit, the Hermit, Bill Peet
Seahorse, Robert A. Morse
Shells from the Sea, Robbie Trent
Houses from the Sea, Alice Goudey

Glue shells onto an empty juice or soup can. Use as a pencil holder. Either use your own shells or purchase some at a craft shop.

Make paper-plate shellfish or fish. Glue small paper plates together, concave sides in. Add features with markers and construction paper.

Let the children taste shrimp or clam chowder.

CHAPTER 17
CHILDREN OF OTHER LANDS OR CULTURES

CHILDREN OF OTHER LANDS OR CULTURES

Because the world is getting "smaller" all the time, it is important that children grow up with an understanding of those of cultures or physical characteristics different from their own. Each culture has its strengths, and this should be emphasized during this unit.

The library, I have found, is a very rich resource. Not only are there books in the children's section with information and pictures on many lands, but numerous books have been written compiling the folktales of individual countries. I have included fiction books written about various peoples, but I urge you to try to find at least one folktale for each day that gives one a feeling for the culture of a country.

Recipe books are also available, if you want to make this unit more elaborate and include more meals for the child or your whole family. The choice, as always, is yours. Also, check the records in your library for native music as well.

This unit is developed around general cultural groups. If you want to spend a day on each country, or perhaps the lands of your ancestors, check the library—there is plenty of material there to do this.

Talk to the children about the fact that the Indians were here upon this continent long before the white man. The Indians were very important to the early settlers in America because they taught them how to hunt wild turkey, plant corn and use dead fish for fertilizer. Through the years, they have been taken advantage of and looked down upon. Some strides have been made, but many more are needed.

Talk about the kinds of clothes that Indians wore in the past. (Remember that they generally do not dress this way now!)

Talk about how they found food and what food they ate: planted corn, which they ground into maize flour; hunted wild animals, such as deer and buffalo, and caught fish; ate berries and roots.

Talk about the fact that they used every part of the animal they had killed—for food, clothing, thongs, moccasins, jewelry, houses (tepees) and weapons. They also had a great knowledge of healing plants and roots.

Little Indian, Peggy Parish
Little Chief, Syd Hoff
Navaho Pet, Patricia M. Martin
Indian Two Feet and the ABC Moose Hunt,
   Margaret Friskey
Little Owl Indian, Hetty Beatty
One Little Indian Boy, Emma Brock
Navaho Stories, Edward Dolch

Indian costumes are easy to make out of brown grocery bags. Draw Indian designs on them with black marker and then let the children color. A few streaks of rouge or eye shadow across their nose and cheeks will complete the picture!

Headband and Feathers: Cut a 2" strip of paper the width of the child's head; tape or staple together. Feathers can be cut from paper, too, or purchased ones from a craft store can be added.

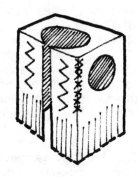

A vest is made from one grocery bag slit up the middle, with appropriate neck and arm openings added. Designs can be drawn on.

An empty oatmeal box makes a perfect drum. Cover the sides with brown construction paper.

A necklace can be made from purchased wooden beads or macaroni colored by shaking in a jar to which you have added ¼ c. colored water to each 1 c. macaroni. Let dry on waxed paper or paper towels overnight. The children can push yarn or string through the openings.

Tepees can be cut out of paper circles. Slit up one side to the center. Color designs around the edge. Overlap sides of slit and glue or tape. A flap opening can be added, too.

Any recipe using corn is appropriate, but here is one for **American Indian Corn Cakes:**

1¼ c. cornmeal
6 T. flour
2 tsp. baking powder
½ tsp. salt
1¼ c. milk
1 egg
3 T. oil

Mix into a thin batter as for pancakes. Use about 2 T. for each cake. Fry on a greased griddle. Makes about 15.

DAY 2
ESKIMOS

Another group found within our own country (Alaska), Greenland, and in the northern regions of North America is the Eskimos. Talk about the barren land where they live and the low temperatures nearly year around.

Talk about what they eat. Since their land is mainly covered with ice and snow, they cannot raise crops. So they live mainly on raw meat (*Eskimo* means "eater of raw meat.") Much of their meat comes from the sea—seal, fish and whale. Whale blubber is like candy to Eskimo children, and it helps them stand the cold. The Eskimos use every part of the animals that they kill for food: fat—fuel; skin and fur—boots, coats and boats; walrus ivory—heads for spears and harpoons.

They sometimes live in snug houses called igloos, made out of snow. They have long tunnels, where their dogs sleep, which lead into the house. The inside is very warm, lit by an oil lamp. Other Eskimos build homes of wood or live in skin tents in the summers.

Eskimos travel by dogsled and by kayak and umiak. Show pictures, if possible.

Ootah's Lucky Day, Peggy Parish
Walpole, Syd Hoff
Beware the Polar Bear, Miriam Young
Little Igloo, Lorraine and Jerrold Beim

Totem poles are fun to make from empty spools, or draw out the design for the children to color on a piece of paper. This can then be glued to an empty paper-towel roll. Since the faces on the totem represent different qualities of the owner, perhaps the children would like pictures to represent them—monkey—curious, bear—strong, lion—brave, etc.

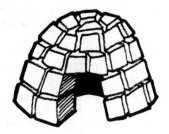

An igloo can be made out of sugar cubes or two layer cakes split in half, plus one cupcake (see Homes—Chapter 4).

Show these countries on a map or globe. Talk about how many of them are hotter than here in the United States. Also, the countries south of the equator have winter when we have summer and vice versa. Point out names of the many countries in this group and have the children try to say them after you.

Explain that there were once many Indians living in South America, just as there were here. Later, people came from other countries—mainly Spain and Portugal. Mention that these are the languages they speak today.

Talk about the kinds of food that the people of these countries eat. Corn, tomatoes, beans and squash are the staples of their diets, in many areas. The Time-Life Cook Books have interesting pictures of the food from these countries: let the children look at them.

Talk about the clothing that they wear. Point out that in big cities, the clothing is similar to what we wear, but in the other areas, the clothes are very unique. Again, library books have interesting pictures of the native costumes.

Let the children hear a record of Mexican or Brazilian music. Talk about the instruments used—guitars and percussion instruments.

Children of the Incas, David Mangurian
The Story of Pancho and the Bull with the Crooked Tail, Berta and Elmer Hader
The Good Llama, Anne Rockwell
Bolivar, Hardie Gramatky
Children are Children are Children: An Activity Approach to Exploring Brazil, France, Iran, Japan, Nigeria and the USSR, Ann Cole et al.

Maracas: Use an empty 6-oz. orange juice can (the kind with the plastic tape opening). Glue bright construction paper to the outside. Add ¼ c. hard beans. Tape top back on. Let the children shake them to the music. (Real maracas have handles, but these little shakers will give the children the idea.)

Make a piñata: blow up a balloon and cover with strips of newspaper passed through a paste of water and flour. Don't put on too many layers, or it will be difficult for the children to break. When dry, either paint or cover with crepe paper. Cut a hole for candy. Hang it from the ceiling. This could be fun for the whole family to break. Blindfold them one at a time, and let them use sticks.

Tacos.

Corn chips dipped in warm refried beans.

DAY 4
EUROPE

Many Americans are of European ancestry.
Point out on a map those countries which were
the homeland for your ancestors (please, apply
this to wherever your family comes from).
Again, have the children repeat the names
after you.

Talk about the many languages that are spoken
in these countries. Pictures from library books
can show the people in their native costumes,
the scenery, etc.

Point out that their food is very similar to ours,
although each country has certain things it is
famous for. Again, use cookbook pictures.

Tito, the Shoeshine Boy, David Mangurian
Madeline series, Ludwig Bemelmans
Paddington series, Michael Bond
Little Toot on the Thames, Hardie Gramatky
Anatole series, Eve Titus
The Hole in the Dike, Norma Green
Anno's Italy, Anno
Anno's Britain, Anno
My Village in Portugal, Sonia and Tim Gidal
My Village in Switzerland, Sonia and Tim Gidal
Children are Children are Children (see Day 3)

Dance to the folk music of these countries.

There are many ideas for costumes in books. They can be simple or elaborate. Here are two ideas from the German-Austrian countries:

Girls: aprons from rectangular doilies taped to a piece of ribbon that will tie around the waist. Hats can be made from round 6'' doilies with several ribbon streamers added to the center.

Boys: suspenders cut from felt or wide ribbon can be pinned to pants or shorts; add felt hearts and flowers if desired.

Nestlé chocolate

Italian food

French pastries

German sausages

Scotch shortbread (Lorna Doone cookies)

French bread

Visit an international food shop and bring home tastes from many places.

Again, show the countries in this continent. Have the children repeat the names after you. Show them that some of the countries are above and some are below the equator. Some of the northern countries are dry and sandy, the middle countries are heavily tropical, and in the south, South Africa has a climate much like the United States.

Show pictures of the people that live in these countries. Often, these people have darker skin. Point out that the blacks in our country were originally brought here from Africa. (This would be a good time to teach them that just because someone's skin is different from ours, we don't treat them unkindly or differently.)

Let them see pictures of what people wear in these lands. Unlike dress in most of the rest of the world, African dress is really very different, and children will want to spend a lot of time talking about what they see.

Talk about the kinds of food they eat—again, use cookbooks.

Talk about the animals that live here and the different perils that the people have from snakes and wild animals.

A is for Africa, Michael Bond
Otto in Africa, William Dubois
Why the Sun and the Moon Live in the Sky, Elphinstone Dayrell
Jambo Means Hello: a Swahili Alphabet Book, Muriel Feelings
Moja Means One: A Swahili Counting Book, Muriel Feelings
The Nuns Go to Africa, Jonathan Routh
Children are Children are Children (see Day 3)

Let them listen to African music on library records.

Make African masks from paper plates.

Since peanuts are from Africa, any treat using them or peanut butter would be appropriate.

DAY 6
ASIA

Show the countries of Asia on a map. Talk about the different sizes of the countries—some are large like China, down to tiny countries like Nepal. Try to have pictures here of the high mountains, the rivers, big cities, etc.

Talk about what they eat: rice, vegetables and fish. Their climate is very wet, so rice grows best here. They eat very little meat because it is very expensive.

Talk about the physical characteristics of these people. There are many different facial features from the Thai to the Mongolians to the Japanese. Also, point out that each country has its very own language and even different languages in the same country.

Talk about the many things that have come to us from Asia, such as fireworks, kites and printing. (Keep this to things that the children can relate to.) Mention that today many of our televisions, radios, and cars come from Japan.

The Five Chinese Brothers, Claire Bishop
The White Wave: a Chinese Tale, Diane
  Wolkstein
A Tiger in the Cherry Tree, Glen Dines
The Village Tree, Jun Iwamatsu
Joji and the Dragon, Betty Lifton
Origami Toys, Toshie Takahama
My Village in Japan, Sonia and Tim Gidal
Children are Children are Children
  (see Day 3)

The children might enjoy briefly listening to some Japanese or other Oriental music. Point out the different sounds these instruments make.

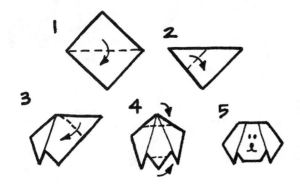

Origami (the art of paper folding) is fun for the children to try and not too difficult with Mother's help. Here is an easy example. (Just be sure to use lightweight paper.)

There are many origami books available that can help you learn more difficult projects, if you're interested. **Origami—Paperfolding for Fun** by Eric Kenneway is especially good.

Fortune cookies

Chow mein noodles

(These are fun served sitting on the floor around a coffee table!)

CHAPTER 18
SPRING

Explain to the children that spring is a season. In spring, the world is changing from winter to summer. The weather starts to get warmer; flowers come up; birds, which have flown south for the winter, begin to return home; the snow melts; the buds begin to swell on the trees; the grass turns green again.

If the weather is good, take them outside to help them find some of the signs of spring mentioned above.

What Happens in Spring, Sandra Brooks
The Boy Who Didn't Believe in Spring, Lucile Clifton
Spring is Like the Morning, M. Jean Craig
Spring Things, Maxine Kumin
Time for Spring, David Leisk
Will Spring Be Early? Crockett Johnson
Spring is Here! Jane Moncure
Hi, Mr. Robin, Alvin Tresselt
Really Spring, Gene Zion
City Springtime, Helen Kay
Spring is a New Beginning, Joan Walsh Anglund

Make an umbrella flowerpot: cut an umbrella shape from construction paper. Glue the bottom (actually the top upside-down) to a piece of paper. Cut small flowers and leaves from brightly colored paper. Glue into the umbrella so that it looks like a flowerpot.

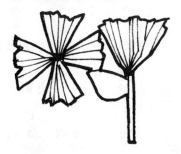

Crepe-Paper Flowers: Cut squares of tissue or crepe paper; gather down the middle. Overlap pieces going in the opposite directions, as many layers as you want. Twist bottoms together. Attach green pipe cleaners. Stand in paper cups filled with rock salt or small pebbles.

Make tissue buds: twist tiny pieces of crepe paper around a small branch to look like flowering buds.

Draw tree outlines on pieces of paper. Let the children color them. Glue individual pieces of tissue to the branches, so that they look like spring blossoms.

DAY 2
THE WIND

On a day with a little wind, have the children outside with you. Have them close their eyes and see if they can feel anything tickling their faces. Ask them if they know what it is. Ask them if they can see the wind.

Put some dry powdered tempera on a piece of paper. Blow it for the children to see. Ask them what happens. Have them try.

Blow up a balloon. Ask the children what is inside. Let the air out for the children to feel. Help them understand that wind is moving air.

Hold a piece of facial tissue by one hand. Blow on it. Try to hold it up by blowing. Let the children try.

Talk about how the wind can be our helper: moves the vanes on windmills, helps boats move, transports seeds, cools us.

When the Wind Blew, Margaret Brown
The Wind Blew, Pat Hutchins
The North Wind and the Sun, Jean De LaFontaine
Who Took the Farmer's Hat? Joan L. Nodset
The March Wind, Inez Rice
Follow the Wind, Alvin Tresselt
When the Wind Stops, Charlotte Zolotow
Curious George Flies a Kite, H. R. Rey
Fish in the Air, Kurt Wiese
Anatole over Paris, Eve Titus
March Wind, Desmond Donnelly

Blow bubbles (use commercial ones or use recipe in Chapter 14).

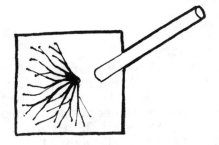

Straw painting: pour a little bright paint on a piece of paper. Let the children make designs by blowing through soda straws.

Make pinwheels: cut squares of construction paper. Cut diagonal slits from corners nearly to the center. Fold each corner in. Push a straight pin or thumbtack through these center corners and attach to the end of a pencil.

Make a kite. Here are some simple, fun ones for children:

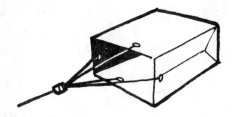

Paper Bag Kite: Draw or paint designs on a large grocery bag. Punch holes on four top edges. Tie a 16" piece of string to each hole. Reinforce with tape. Join other ends and attach to flying string. This won't fly high, but will sail behind a running child. (This also works with a plastic garbage bag.)

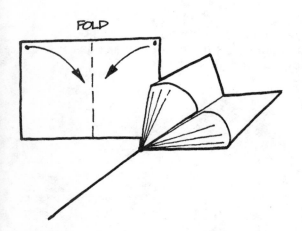

FOLD

Tot Kite: Decorate or color a piece of 9"x12" lightweight paper. (Construction paper, for example, is too heavy.) Fold in half. Bring two corners toward the center fold and staple or tape down. Do not crease. Turn kite over and attach a piece of string through a hole punched in the pointed end.

Hold a white sponge over a pan. Tell the children to pretend that this is a cloud. Pour some water into it. Pour until the water begins to seep through the sponge and fall into the pan. Ask the children what this is.

Help the children understand that rain comes when the clouds are too full of water. When it falls, it seeps into the ground and "disappears" or forms puddles which evaporate back up into the sky.

Show rain clothes to the children. Name each item and talk about how it keeps us dry. Have the children put on the clothes. (If you don't have rain gear, use pictures and pretend to put on the clothes.)

Collect some rainwater and let the children taste it.

My Red Umbrella, Robert Bright
Umbrella, Taro Yashima
Rain Drop Splash, Alvin Tresselt
All Falling Down, Gene Zion
The Storm Book, Charlotte Zolotow
Where Does the Butterfly Go When it Rains?
  May Garelick
The Good Rain, Alice Goudey
Johnny Lion's Rubber Boots, Edith Hurd
Rain, Robert Kalan.
When It Rains, Mary Kwitz
And It Rained, Evelyn Raskin

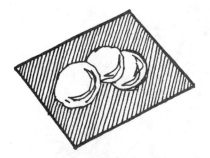

Make cloud pictures by gluing cotton balls onto blue paper.

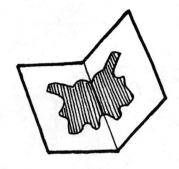

Ink-Blot Pictures: Drop blobs of ink onto a piece of paper. Fold paper in half. Open and let dry.

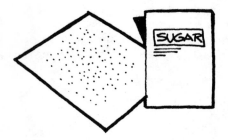

Colored Sugar Pictures: Sprinkle a piece of paper with either colored sugar purchased from the store, or sugar that you have colored with dry tempera paint powder. Set the paper out in a drizzle for just a minute until damp. Let dry.

Paint with a wet sponge dipped in dry tempera powder.

CHAPTER 19
FLOWERS AND PLANTS

DAY 1
WHAT ARE PLANTS?

Bring a branch from an early budding bush or tree. Let the children see and feel the buds. Place in water near the window. As leaves emerge, have them notice the size, shape and color.

Talk about where plants come from. A seed is a plant that has not started to grow. When the seed is moistened, a root starts to grow. Little roots grow from the big root; they look like tiny hairs. They are called root hairs. Soon a shoot pushes through the ground. It is the beginning of a green plant. The shoot turns green. It grows toward the sun. The leaves come next. Then, flowers follow. (This works best for me if I draw a picture as I am talking about the seed becoming a plant.)

In My Garden, Charlotte Zolotow
Jack and the Beanstalk (various authors)
Seeds and More Seeds, Millicent Selsam
Mushroom in the Rain, Mirra Ginsberg
Seeds by Wind and Water, Helene Jordan

Here is one green leaf, *(Hold up one hand cupping fingers.)*
And here is another. *(Hold up other hand.)*
Soon you'll have a little flower *(Cup hands together.)*
To give to your mother! *(Open hands up slowly like a flower.)*

I will plant a little seed
In the ground so deep. *(Pretend to plant a seed.)*
I will water it so the seed *(Pretend to water it.)*
Will no longer sleep.
Roots down, stem up—*(Spread fingers down, then reach arms up.)*
It grows every hour.
Then one day I look,
And I see a flower. *(Cup hands together like a flower.)*

Place several bean seeds between moistened sheets of paper toweling. Cover with plastic wrap to keep the moisture in. Place in a dark place. As the week continues, let the children see the root appear, etc.

Make a collage from pictures cut from a seed catalog.

Make tiny flowerpots: cut pieces of colored sponges into flower shapes. Stick onto green pipe cleaner stems. Cut leaves from construction paper. Pots can be empty painted spools, or tiny ones can be made with the tops from toothpaste tubes filled with modeling clay.

Make a picture out of different kinds of seeds. Trace your design onto paper. Place the seeds on. Then glue in place.

Eat vegetables and talk about how they grow from plants.

Eat alfalfa sprouts in a salad.

DAY 2
WHAT DO PLANTS NEED TO GROW?

Take a piece of celery. Place into a glass containing water that you have colored with red or blue food coloring. In just a few minutes, the water will begin to be absorbed through the veins. Explain that this is the way a plant takes in the food it eats, through the "veins."

Show the children a plant that you've allowed to dry out. Talk about the wilted leaves. Water it. Let the children see through the day how the leaves become firmer and stronger.

Show the children how a plant will grow toward the sunlight. If you don't have indoor plants, take them outside and let them see.

Blue Bug's Vegetable Garden, Virginia Poulet
Green is for Growing, Winifred Lubell
The Plant Setter, Gene Zion
The Turnip, A. Tolstoy
Let's Grow Things, Deborah Manley

When the flowers are thirsty, *(Hold hands out like flowers.)*
And the grass is dry, *(Hold hands out flat.)*
Merry little raindrops tumble from the sky. *(Fingers patter.)*
All around they patter *(Tap fingers on a table.)* In their happy play,
Till the little sunbeams *(Fold arms in a circle above your head.)*
Chase them all away. *(Wave hands "good-bye.")*

The sun comes out and shines so bright, *(arms above head)*
Then we have a shower. *(Wiggle fingers down like rain.)*
The little bud pushes with all its might, *(Push arms up.)*
And soon we have a flower. *(Open hands like a flower opening.)*

Make a carrot plant: cut about two inches off the top of a carrot. Put some wet gravel in a small margarine tub; place the carrot top in the gravel. The water should be level with the bottom of the carrot. Soon, it will become a plant.

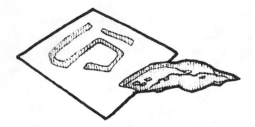

Make a design out of glue on a piece of paper. Sprinkle loose potting soil over it. Shake off the excess.

Place small, flat flowers between pieces of waxed paper. (The flowers from spring-blossoming trees are nice.) Iron and cut to make bookmarks. (Punch a hole in the top of each bookmark and tie a ribbon on, if you want.)

DAY 3
GROWING PLANTS

This day is mainly an activity day. Here are a few books:

The Carrot Seed, Robert Krauss
The Little Red Flower, Paul Tripp
Let's Grow a Garden, Gyo Fujikawa

Make a terrarium out of a large glass bowl or jar (glass canisters are nice). Sprinkle in a layer of gravel or small rocks, a layer of charcoal, then about two inches of fine soil. Plant with several small house plants. A small glass figurine is nice to add, too. Spray with water and replace the top. If the sides become too humid, the top can be opened for an hour or so. If the plants are too dry, spray one or two times.

Make an eggshell garden: cut the top off an egg carton. Place rinsed and dried eggshell halves into the carton. Fill with a small amount of soil. Add a few seeds to each shell (herb seeds or marigolds work nicely). Dampen soil thoroughly. Cover with plastic wrap to keep the soil moist. Place the carton in a warm, dark place until the seeds begin to sprout. Then remove the wrap and place in the sun. When tall enough, they can be planted in the garden, eggshell and all.

Avocado plants are easy to start, too. Poke toothpicks through the sides of the seed. Suspend in a glass of water with the flat side at the bottom, just touching the water. Keep in light, but out of sun, until rooted, then move into sun. When taproot is 4-5 inches long, transplant to a pot of soil. In about a month, a shoot will appear (it takes a long time!). When 2 feet tall, pinch off tip.

Visit a greenhouse or florist to view the many kinds of plants and flowers.

Plant purchased plants or flowers outdoors for the summer. The children might like to have their own plot to take care of.

CHAPTER 20
EASTER

DAY 1
WHAT IS EASTER?

Easter in the Christian world is the celebration of the resurrection of Christ, and everyone handles this differently in relationship to the "Easter bunny" and the secular trappings of Easter. For this reason, this unit will involve only the nonreligious side of Easter.

In our own family, we do talk about the bunny, who pays his visit to our home on Saturday. We then continue the rest of the holiday in religious worship. Like Christmas, feel free to handle this in the best way for your family.

Bring an Easter basket, either a special family basket or a purchased one, and let the children put Easter grass and colored or plastic eggs into it. Explain why they are doing this.

Cut out different-colored eggs and rabbits from construction paper and let the children match them by color. As an extra reinforcement, ask them to bring you the "blue egg" or the "green basket."

Hide paper eggs throughout the room. Let the children see how many they can find.

The Egg Tree, Katherine Milhous
Golden Egg Book, Margaret Brown
Jennie's Hat, Ezra Keats
Lillies, Rabbits and Painted Eggs, Edna Barth
The World in the Candy Egg, Alvin Tresselt

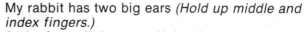

My rabbit has two big ears *(Hold up middle and index fingers.)*
And a funny little nose. *(Join other three fingers for nose.)*
He likes to nibble carrots, *(Wiggle the three fingers.)*
And he hops wherever he goes. *(Move your hand up and down.)*

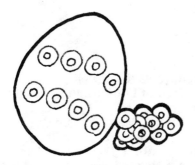

Make Easter cards for friends or relatives: pictures can be colored on cards, cut from old cards that you have saved or cut from Easter wrapping paper.

Egg-shaped cards are fun to make, too. Cut an egg from colored construction paper and let the children decorate it with gummed reinforcements (available at an office supply store). Children love to lick, and they can make lots of designs.

Make little eggshell Easter nests: blow out an egg and cut off the top third. Paint with tempera or watercolors. Fill with Easter grass or cotton balls. Cut a little chicken out of yellow construction paper and sit it in the nest. The egg can stand up on a five-inch circle that you have slit, cut an inch circle in and formed into a cone.

Cut out a bunny. Put each piece on a board, one at a time, adding the ears last. Let them guess what it is.

Bring a real bunny to visit. Perhaps you have a friend or neighbor who can bring in their pet. (If not, most pet stores have pet rabbits at Easter time.)

Talk about rabbits: how soft their fur is, how their long ears help them hear well, what big back legs rabbits have and smaller front ones to help them jump and run quickly, the things that rabbits like to eat (fruits, vegetables, grass).

Have the children pretend that they are bunnies. Let them hop around and wiggle their noses, if they can.

Snuggle Bunny, Nancy Jewell
The Adventures of Little Rabbit, retold by Janet Fulton
Home for a Bunny, Margaret Brown
The Runaway Bunny, Margaret Brown
The Velveteen Rabbit, Margery Williams
A Rabbit has a Habbit, Jane Moncure
The Tale of Peter Rabbit, Beatrix Potter
Carrot Nose, Jan Wahl
Mother Rabbit's Son Tom, Dick Gackenbach
Here Comes Peter Cottontail, Steve Nelson
Humbug Rabbit, Lorna Balian

This little bunny has two pink eyes. *(Bend down fourth finger.)*
This little bunny is very wise. *(Bend down third finger.)*
This little bunny has fur so white. *(Bend down second finger.)*
This little bunny will hop out of sight. *(Bend down index finger.)*
This little bunny's ears bend and sway. *(Bend down thumb.)*
Five little bunnies who hop and play. *(Extend thumb and fingers back out straight and have them jump around.)*

Here's a bunny with ears so funny. *(two fingers up and bent)*
Here's his hole in the ground. *(Make circle with thumb and index finger of other hand.)*
When a noise he hears, he pricks up his ears, *(Straighten fingers.)*
And jumps in the hole in the ground. *(Jump the bunny into the circle.)*

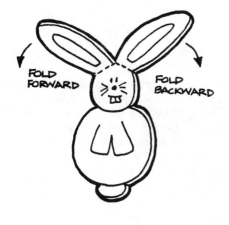

Make a twirly bunny out of heavy paper and let the children color it. Fold one ear forward and one back. Stand bunny on a chair or at the top of your stairs and let it twirl down.

Make a rabbit out of different-sized hearts cut out of pink construction paper. Draw on features.

Make an egg rabbit, using a plastic panty hose container. Glue on eyes and ears cut from felt. Whiskers can be made from broom straws or stiff twine. Add a cotton-ball tail.

Let the children color a large paper rabbit picture, such as this one. This can be used on the party day to play "Pin the Tail on the Bunny."

Make Easter bunny buns: prepare hot roll mix as directed on package. Then, take a 12"x1" strip of dough, overlapping the ends to form two circles and ears. Add a small ball for the tail. Let rise until double. Bake at 375 degrees about 12 minutes. Frost with a powdered-sugar-and-milk glaze. Add raisin eyes.

Make cookies using three slices of refrigerator cookie dough: two round ones for the head and body, and one round one sliced in half for the ears. Add raisin eyes.

Using a commercial cookie cutter, make bunny cookies.

Eat carrots and lettuce, as rabbits do.

DAY 3
LET'S HAVE AN EASTER PARTY

Make bunny ears for each child by stapling long pink ears cut from construction paper, to a paper headband.

Play "Pin the Tail on the Bunny," using the pattern from Day 2, and have the children attach cotton balls with tape on the back.

Sing or play the record "Here Comes Peter Cottontail." The children can hop around to the music. Or teach them how to play musical chairs.

Make Jellied Easter Eggs:

2 pkg. fruit-flavored gelatin
2 pkg. unflavored gelatin
3 c. boiling water
12 eggs

Break shells of eggs carefully so that just the tip of the shell is broken and the egg is removed. (Use the eggs for breakfast!) Dissolve all gelatin in the boiling water. Cool. Place empty shells in egg carton and fill with gelatin mixture. Chill at least 3 hours or until well set. Roll eggs gently on table to crack shells; peel carefully. Refrigerate.

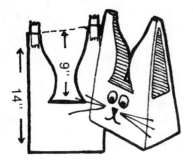

Make a rabbit basket to hold Easter candy.
Here are three ideas:

Bunny Egg Bag: Take a grocery bag 14" long,
measure down 9" and draw a line across the
bag. Draw curved lines (as shown) from the
two corners down to this line. Make round
eyes, a triangle nose and a curvy mouth.
Whiskers are pipe cleaners or soda straws
bent in half and taped on. With the bag still
closed, cut the ears along the lines you've
drawn. Tape the tops of the ears together.

Margarine Basket: Cut bunny head pattern, as
shown, out of brown construction paper. Have
the children color on features. Glue onto the
side of a plastic margarine tub (the small size
is best). Punch holes with a paper punch on
the two opposite sides. Attach a pipe-cleaner
handle with paper fasteners. Glue on a
cotton-ball tail.

Milk Carton: Cut the top off an 8-oz. milk
carton, leaving the sides two inches high. Glue
cotton balls all around the outside. Add 3" ears
cut from white cardboard and lined with pink
felt. Make the face with wiggly eyes, a pompon
nose, pink felt tongue and wire-flower-stamen
whiskers.

CHAPTER 21
INSECTS

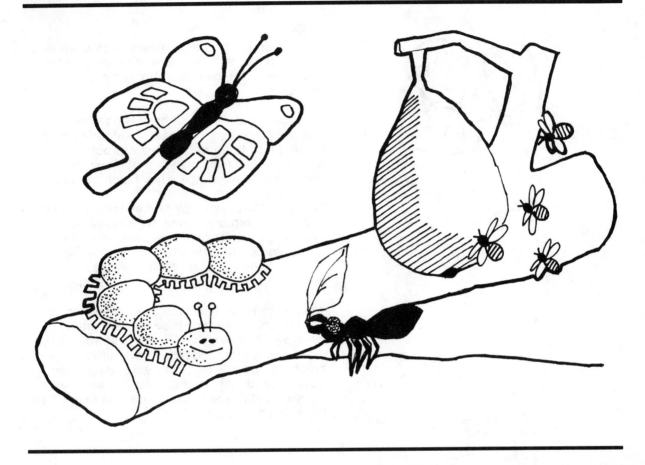

DAY 1
WHAT ARE INSECTS?

Show pictures of lots of insects. Ask what they are. Help the children learn the names of the main ones: ant, bee, ladybug, butterfly, caterpillar.

Talk about the things all insects have in common: six legs, one pair of antennas, a body divided into three parts, a waterproof body. Most have big eyes made up of many little ones. Most have wings. They hatch from eggs.

Talk about the way their bodies are colored and shaped to help them hide: walking sticks look like tree twigs; grasshoppers are green like grass; some butterflies have large "eye spots" on their wings to scare their enemies; measuring worms look like broken sticks.

Tell the children that even though insects sometimes look scary, they are very interesting when we look closely at them. Butterflies have many lovely colors. Beetles have different numbers of spots on their backs. Help them learn to study the insects that they see, being careful to stay away from those that might hurt them, such as bees.

A Book of Bugs, Haris Pelie
Fresh Cider and Pie, Franz Brandenberg
Blue Bug series, Virginia Poulet
The Bears' Nature Guide, Stan and Jan
    Berenstain, pp. 40-41
Look at Insects, Harriet Huntington
A First Look at Insects, Millicent Selsam
The Grouchy Ladybug, Eric Carle

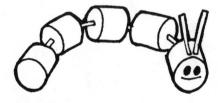

Make caterpillars using Tootsie Roll sections or little marshmallows, hooked together with toothpicks. Use cloves for eyes and toothpicks for antennas.

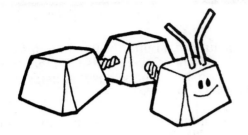

Make caterpillars from three sections of the bottom of an egg carton. Add pipe-cleaner antennas and marker eyes. You can add another section of three attached with yarn to make a centipede.

Eat your Tootsie Roll caterpillars.

Ants on a Log: Fill a stalk of celery with peanut butter. Dot the top with raisins (ants).

Show a picture of a butterfly. Point out the eyes, body, antennas, wings. Mention that there is a special dust on their wings that helps the butterflies fly.

Discuss the differences between butterflies and moths: butterflies usually fly in the daytime—moths at night; butterflies rest with their wings up—moths with their wings flat; butterflies have slender bodies—moths are plump and often look furry; butterflies have slender antennas—moths' antennas look like feathers.

With the help of a library book, show the life cycle of a butterfly. First, it lays eggs, which hatch into larvas or caterpillars; next comes the pupa or sleepy stage (butterflies make chrysalises, moths—cocoons); when this splits open, the adult butterfly appears.

The Butterfly, A. Delaney
Very Hungry Caterpillar, Eric Carle
ABC Butterflies, Marcia Brown
The Butterfly Collector, Naomi Lewis
The Butterfly, Paula J. Hogan
Our Caterpillars, Herbert Wong and Matthew Vessel

Make butterfly clothespins: cut multicolors of tissue paper into 6'' squares. Pinch together through the center and attach to clothespin. Cut a pipe cleaner in half and glue onto the top for antennas.

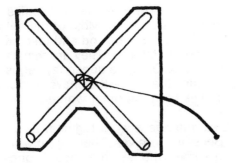

Make a butterfly kite: glue two drinking straws together in the middle. Lay onto a sheet of paper and cut out as shown. Color the paper so that it looks like a butterfly. Lay a two-foot piece of string across the middle of the kite, with three inches on one side, the rest on the other. Glue the straws and the string to the paper. Tie the string into a knot. Hold onto the string and fly your kite.

Make butterfly sandwiches: make a sandwich with the child's favorite filling. Cut the bread from corner to corner in both directions. Cut a carrot into one long and two short strips. Place on a plate with the bread "wings" along the sides.

Ants: Talk about how they live in colonies and work together as a group. Most of the ants are worker ants: they gather food and take care of the queen and baby ants. They are females but do not lay eggs. Only the queen lays eggs. Soldiers guard the nest—they have bigger and stronger jaws than the other workers.

Bees: Like ants, bees work together as a group. Bees live in hives. There is only one queen in a hive who lays the eggs. Drones are male bees. Most of the hive is made up of workers—females—who do not lay eggs. The workers gather nectar for honey and pollen. Some make honeycomb wax out of their bodies to store the honey, some take care of the queen, some feed the baby bees, some fan the air, some keep the hive clean and some guard the hive. A few baby bees are fed a special food called royal jelly; they become queens. When a young queen bee grows up, the old queen leaves with many workers to make a new hive.

Here Come the Bees! Alice Goudey
Buzz, Buzz, Buzz, Byron Barton
Bees, Wasps and Hornets, Robert M. McClung
Follow Me, Cried Bee, Jan Wahl
Little Lost Bee, Joan Kapral
Ants are Fun, Mildred Myrick
The Ant and the Elephant, Bill Peet
The Ants Go Marching, Berniece Freschet

Here is the hive, *(Hold hands together to make hive.)*
But where are the bees?
They're hiding inside, *(Pretend to look inside.)*
As quiet as you please.
Now look at the bees coming out of the hive.
1,2,3,4,5—*(Hold up fingers one at a time.)*
Buzz!

Ant Farm in a Jar: Place a small clean glass jar upside-down inside a large clean glass jar. (This will keep the ants confined around the outside of the glass, so that you can see them). Fill the space between the jars with loose or sandy soil. Locate some ants and make an ant trap by mixing a little sugar and water in a small jar and laying it on its side near the anthill. When you have about 20 ants, place them inside the large jar and cap it or cover with plastic wrap. In a day or two, the ants will begin to build tunnels. Once a week, feed the ants a few drops of sugar-water and maybe a few grains of bird or grass seed. Don't overfeed the ants. Keep the jar at room temperature away from the heat and fairly shaded.

Make a beehive pin holder: cut the bottom off a Styrofoam egg, so that it will stand. Make a small hole in the top of the egg. Insert the end of a giftwrap cord or narrow macrame cord; glue and secure with a pin. Apply glue to top section of egg and begin wrapping cord in spiral. Apply more glue as each section is covered. Decorate finished hive with artificial flowers or a tiny bee.

Make honey candy or taffy. Here's an easy recipe:

2 c. honey
1 c. sugar
1 c. cream or evaporated milk

Combine ingredients and cook slowly to hard ball stage. Pour onto buttered platter, and when cool enough to handle, grease or butter hands and pull until a golden color. Cut into pieces.

CHAPTER 22
FARMS

DAY 1
WHAT IS A FARM?

Show a picture of a farm. Ask the children what it is. Help them learn the names for the farmhouse, barn, fences, chicken house.

Help the children learn where the different animals sleep on the farm. The horses and cows sleep in the barns, the chickens in the chicken house, the pigs in little houses in the pigsty, the sheep in the sheep fold outside.

Talk about the things that they could do if they lived on a farm: help feed the chickens, gather eggs, milk the cows, pitch hay, hoe the garden, etc. They could pantomime doing these different activities.

Tim Mouse Visits the Farm, Judy Brook
Over the River and Through the Woods, Lydia Child
I Know a Farm, Ethel Collier
Grandpa's Farm, James Flora
Bright Barnyard, Dahlov Ipcar
The Year at Maple Hill Farm, Alice and Martin Provensen
Blue Barns, Helen Sewell
The Barn, John Schoenharr
Wake Up, Farm, Alvin Tresselt
Little Farm, Lois Lenski
Big Red Barn, Eve Bunting
Big Red Barn, Margaret Brown

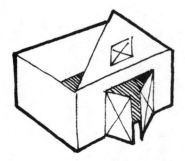

Barn: With red tempera paint, paint a box, shoe size or larger. A red triangle from poster paper can be taped on one end to make a false loft. Use white paint to outline a door and loft windows. The double door can be cut open as shown.

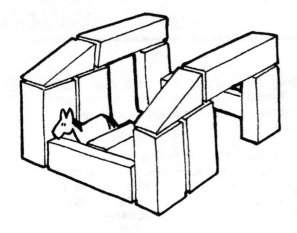

With blocks, build a barn. Small blocks can be used to make partitions (stalls) for the horses and cows.

DAY 2
WHAT DO FARMERS DO?

Talk about the jobs a farmer does: planting, hoeing, feeding the animals, milking the cows, mending fences. Let the children imitate these jobs.

Talk about the tools that help a farmer. Try to have a picture of a tractor. Have the children try to guess what he is going to plant with the tractor. Talk about other tools generally found on farms: a pitchfork, a plow, a harvester.

If I Drove a Tractor, Miriam Young
Who Took the Farmer's Hat? Joan Lexau
The Little Farmer, Margaret Brown
Farmer Barnes and the Goats, Joan Cunliffe
Farmer in the Dell, illustrated by Diane
  Zuromskis
Farmer Palmer's Wagon Ride, William Steig

"The Farmer in the Dell"

"Little Boy Blue, Come Blow Your Horn"

Visit a farm to watch what the farmer does.

Visit a dairy to watch the cows being milked.

Make butter from whipping cream; serve on bread.

Show pictures of farm animals; tell something about each one. Help the children learn the sounds that the animals make. (Use pigs, cows, sheep, horses, ducks, geese, goats, chickens and roosters.)

As you hold up a picture of an animal, have the children tell you what it is. Go through the pictures again and have the children tell you the sound that each makes.

Talk about the food that comes from each animal.

The Little Duck, Judy Dunn
The Little Goat, Judy Dunn
The Little Lamb, Judy Dunn
Horses, Margaret Brown
Petunia series, Roger Duvoisin
The Story of a Little Red Rooster, Berta and
    Elmer Hader
One Horse Farm, Ipcar Dahlov
Small Pig, Arnold Lobel
Friendly Farm Animals, Esther Meeks
Our Animal Friends, Alice and Martin
    Provensen
Look at a Calf, Dave Wright
Look at a Colt, Dave Wright
Farmyard Animals, Jean Wilson
Horses, Janusz Grabianski

"Mary had a Little Lamb"

"Baa, Baa, Black Sheep"

Make a little farm animal book by placing stickers on pages of a little paper book.

Color little pictures of farm animals. Mount on cardboard. Cut half circles from cardboard for stand. Make a slit halfway down. Cut a corresponding size in the base of the picture. When placed at right angles, the picture will stand. Put them in and around the barn you made on Day 1.

Eat food from farm animals, for example, eggs, milk, bacon.

CHAPTER 23
THE ZOO AND WILD ANIMALS

Show pictures of many familiar wild animals (such as elephants, monkeys, lions, tigers, giraffes, bears, zebras, crocodiles). Help the children learn their names. Talk about each one, discussing its shape, size, color and habitat.

Play an animal guessing game: hold up a picture and have the children tell you what it is. Then display all the pictures, name one and have the children point to it.

Play animal charades: imitate an animal and have the children guess what it is. After a while they will want to do this and have you guess.

Henry Explores the Jungle, Mark Taylor
In the Jungle, Eugene Booth
In the Forest, Marie Ets
Animal Babies, Harry McNaught
Animals Everywhere, Ingri and Edgar D'Aulaire
Animals, Anno
Animals, Lois Lenski
Animal Babies, Max Zoll
The Big Book of Wild Animals, Felix Sutton
About Animals, Richard Scarry
Animal Babies, Ylla
Wild Animals: From Alligator to Zebra, Arthur Singer
Grabianski's Wild Animals, Janusz Grabianski

Make a paper book: have the children glue in pictures and lick stamps or stickers of wild animals.

Make a lotto game: divide several 9" cardboard squares into 3" squares. Glue pictures of different animals in each square. Cut smaller 3" square cards; glue corresponding pictures to them. Draw the cards out and let the children try to match them with their larger squares. (The pictures can either be drawn on or you can use animal stickers.)

Animal Puzzles: Have the children color animal pictures (coloring books are good sources). Cover the back with spray adhesive and press down on a piece of contruction paper or light cardboard. Cut into about five large pieces. Let the children try to make them into a picture again.

What better day for animal crackers!

Hold up a picture of an elephant. Let the children tell you what it is.

Talk about the different parts of the elephant and what they are used for:
Trunk—picking up objects, picking up food, filling with water for a bath.
Ears—big and floppy; African elephants have bigger ears than Indian ones.
Tusks—used by the elephant for protection; used by people to make jewelry and piano keys; made of ivory.
Large, strong legs—important to help hold up the elephant.
Tough hide—protection from insects and the jungle.

Talk about what elephants eat: they are plant eaters, gathering grass with their trunks and digging up roots with their tusks. They can also drink up to 50 gallons of water a day.

Little Wild Elephant, Anne Michel
Did Anyone See My Elephant? Robert Leydenfrol
If I Rode an Elephant, Miriam Young
The Elephant's Visit, Bob Bauer
The Elephant Who Wanted to be a Leopard, Eve Witte
Baby Elephant series, Sesyle Joslin
Babar the Elephant series, Laurent and Jean de Brunhoff
Horton Hatches the Egg, Dr. Seuss
The Smallest Elephant in the World, Alvin Tresselt
Little Elephant, Arthur Gregor
Ah-choo, Mercer Mayer
The Ant and the Elephant, Bill Peet

March like elephants to a record. The "Elephant Patrol" from the *The Jungle Book* by Walt Disney is a good one.

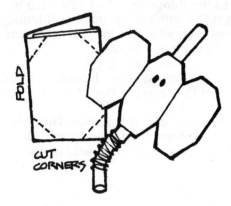

Make elephants on straws: fold a piece of construction paper into thirds, cut small triangles off the top two sides and larger triangles off the bottom. Open up and draw eyes on center section. Tape a soda straw to the back. When the children hold on to the straw and wave it up and down, the elephant's ears will flop.

Make an elephant pencil holder: cover an empty soup can with grey paper. Add paper ears and trunk. Color on eyes.

Eat peanuts, as the elephants in the zoo do.

Talk about the wild members of the cat family: lions, tigers, leopards, jaguars and others. (We will be talking about tame ones in the next chapter.)

Show pictures and help the children tell the differences between the different cats. The colors will be the biggest difference that they will notice.

Talk about the things that wild cats have in common (even with house cats): cushioned paws, meat diet, whiskers that act as feelers, excellent hearing and sight.

The lion is the largest "cat." It lives in Africa and is called the "King of Beasts."

Another familiar "cat" is the tiger. They are striped to help them hide in tall grass. Unlike the lions, they are only found wild in Asia.

The Happy Lion series, Louise Fatio
Tigers in the Cellar, Carol Fenner
The Story of Little Black Sambo, Helen Bannerman
The Sleepy Little Lion, Margaret Brown
Johnny Lion series, Edith Hurd
Hubert's Hair Raising Adventure, Bill Peet
Leo the Late Bloomer series, Robert Kraus
The Rat and the Lion, Jean De LaFontaine
The Terrible Tiger, Jack Prelutsky
The Tiger Hunt, Mary Villarejo
Here Come the Lions! Alice Goudey

Make a lion container: cover an empty juice can with gold felt. On the top, glue small pieces of yarn for the mane. Cut a piece of yarn for the tail and glue on. Cut a circle of felt the size of the can lid for the face; glue over yarn. Use pipe cleaners for the whiskers. For eyes, glue small black felt circles inside small white buttons (or use "wiggly" eyes). This can also be made with a shortening can and used to hold crayons or markers.

Show pictures of monkeys. Have the children tell you what they are.

Talk about the things that monkeys do: use their tails to swing from trees; use their fingers to pick fruit and peel it; live together in groups.

Talk about what monkeys eat: fruits and vegetables.

Have the children act out being monkeys.

Run Little Monkeys, Run, Run, Run, Juliet Kepes
Babar and Zephir, Laurent de Brunhoff
The Monkey and the Crocodile, Paul Galdone
Jacko, John S. Goodall
Arthur series, Russell Hoban
Five Little Monkeys, Juliet Kepes
Curious George series, H. A. Rey
Monkey Tale, Hamilton Williamson

Make a jumping monkey: enlarge the pieces shown and cut out; glue to cardboard; join pieces loosely with paper fasteners; tape or glue a tongue depressor behind the head. When you bounce the depressor up and down, the monkey will jump.

Make a monkey mask, using a paper plate. Cut to fit child's head. Add string ties to attach behind the head. Paint or color appropriate colors.

Eat peanuts or bananas.

DAY 5
BEARS

Show a picture of a bear. Ask the children what it is.

Show pictures of different kinds of bears and talk about where they live: polar bears—northern climates; brown and black bears—mountain forests. You might also want to talk about koalas and pandas; even though they aren't really bears, everyone calls them bears. (Koalas live in Australia; pandas, in China.)

Talk about what bears eat: bugs, berries, honey and sometimes meat.

Talk about what bears do in the winter—hibernate (sleep).

Bears have big appetites, and bears in zoos often do tricks to get something to eat. They can be trained to dance and perform in circuses because they can stand on their hind legs.

The Marshmallow Caper, Gloria Miklowitz
Winnie the Pooh, A. A. Milne
Berenstain Bears series, Stan and Jan Berenstain
Paddington series, Michael Bond
Brimhall series, Judy Delton
Ask Mr. Bear, Marjorie Flack
Nobody Listens to Andrew, Elizabeth Guiloile
Milton the Early Riser, Robert Kraus
Buzzy Bear series, Dorothy Marino
Little Bear series, Else Minarik
The Bear Who Had No Place to Go, James Stevenson
Mr. Bear and the Robbers, Chizuko Kuratomi
Beware the Polar Bear, Miriam Young
The Bear's Toothache, David McPhail
Not This Bear! Bernice Meyers
The Lazy Bear, Brian Wildsmith
Goldilocks and the Three Bears (various authors)

Take your bears on a "Teddy Bear" picnic in a park or just in your own backyard. Be sure to bring lots of bear food—ants on a log (see Chapter 21), bread and honey, etc.

Make a climbing bear: enlarge the bear pattern to about 5" and cut two out of cardboard. Cut two pieces of string 3' long and tie to a 6" dowel or piece of coat hanger. Glue the two bears together, leaving a channel for the string to run through the arms as shown. When the dowel is held by one person or hung over a door knob, the bear will "climb" as the strings are pulled. (You can also make a wooden version of this bear. Use only one pattern and drill holes for the strings.)

Talk about what a zoo is—a place where many animals are kept so that we can go to see them.

In many zoos today, the animals are not kept in cages behind bars but are in their natural environments. They are separated from the people by deep gullies, wire fences or water. This is nice for the animals because they can feel more at home in a zoo, and we can see them doing many of the things that they would do if they were out in the wild.

Talk about the rules of a zoo, e.g., don't feed the animals unless the zoo allows it; don't lean over partitions or climb fences; don't throw things at the animals.

Again, review the names of many animals by showing the pictures and letting them say the names.

If I Ran the Zoo, Theodor Geisel
Zoo Babies, Donna Grosvenor
What If a Lion Eats Me and I Fall in a Hippopotamus' Mud Hole? Emily Hanlon
Zoo City, Stephen Lewis
Something New at the Zoo, Esther Meeks
One Day at the Zoo, Dick Snyder
George and Martha series, James Marshall
There's a Hippopotamus Under My Bed, Mike Thaler
"You Look Ridiculous," said the Rhinoceros to the Hippo, Bernard Waber
We Visit the Zoo, Bruce Wannamaker
The Giant Giraffe, Eve Holmquist
Come to the Zoo, Ruth M. Jansen
Zoo Animals, Leonard Shortall

Visit a local zoo. If you don't have one, perhaps there is a petting farm or a "traveling zoo" in your area that you can arrange to see.

Make a zoo: draw animal pictures on the sides of small boxes. Arrange the boxes in groups to form a zoo.

Make animal masks out of paper plates (like the monkey mask on Day 4).

Make egg carton critters: (here are two ideas—use your own).

CHAPTER 24
PETS

DAY 1
DOGS

Show pictures of different kinds of dogs. (Libraries have lots of books.)

Talk about the sizes of dogs. Talk about the colors and the different kinds of hair in their coats.

Talk about what dogs do to help: collies and sheep dogs help shepherds; retrievers and other hunting dogs help hunters find and capture game and wild birds; St. Bernards are used to find lost climbers; German Shepherds help the police and blind people.

Talk about the kind of food that dogs eat. Make a point of helping the children understand that "people food," especially sweets, is harmful to a dog.

Talk about the other things that must be done to help take care of dogs: giving them water; providing a place for them to sleep; taking them to a vet to get their shots, which protect them from disease; making sure that they get enough exercise; brushing their coats and having their hair trimmed as needed.

Harry the Dog series, Gene Zion
Go, Dog, Go, P. D. Eastman
The Big Book of Dogs, Felix Sutton
Claude, the Dog, Dick Gackenbach
Pete's Pup: 3 Puppy Stories, Syd Hoff
Dogs, Camille Koffler

Visit a pet store and look at the dogs. Talk about the different kinds.

If you don't own a dog, arrange a visit with a friend who does. Have them show you where their dog sleeps, what he eats and other aspects of his lifestyle.

Make a doggy mobile. Fold a piece of brown paper in half and cut as shown. Open up and hang down two black button eyes. Attach a string to the top and hang from doorway or ceiling.

Make sugar cookies or cut slices of bread in the shape of dog biscuits. Let the children pretend that they are doggies eating their dinner.

DAY 2
CATS

Handle this day much as you did the day on Dogs. Talk about what clean animals cats are, always grooming themselves. Cats are easy to care for, since they can look after themselves better than most pets.

Talk about the way cats make purring noises when they are happy or contented. Talk about the cat's paws and how the claws can be extended for protection (to scratch another animal or climb a tree).

Talk about what cats eat. Farmers like to have cats around their barns to catch mice and rats. Cats also like to catch birds, which makes many people unhappy.

The Big Book of Cats, Gladys Cook
Kittens for Nothing, Robert Kraus
Catch that Cat, Fernando Krahn
Find the Cat, Elaine Livermore
Convent Cat, Barbara Willard
Grandmother Lucy's Cat series, Joyce Wood
Katy's Kitty: 3 Kitty Stories, Syd Hoff
Cats, Camille Koffler

There once were two cats of Kilkenny.
Each thought there was one cat too many.
So they fought and they fit,
And they scratched and they bit
Till, excepting their nails
And the tips of their tails,
Instead of two cats, there weren't any.

The three little kittens, they lost their mittens,
And they began to cry,
"Oh, Mother dear, we sadly fear, our mittens we have lost."
"What, lost your mittens? You naughty kittens,
Now you shall have no pie."
The three little kittens, they found their mittens,
And they began to cry,
"Oh, Mother dear, see here, see here. Our mittens we have found."
"What, found your mittens? You darling kittens,
Now you shall have some pie."

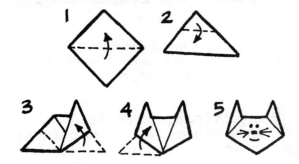

Make an origami cat. (Flip paper over between steps 4 and 5.) Draw on face.

Make a spool cat: enlarge pattern, color, and glue to ends of an empty spool of thread.

Eat Goldfish crackers.

Children also think it is fun to lick milk out of a saucer as kittens do.

Have the children think of some other animals that their friends have as pets, for example, hamsters, gerbils, mice, fish, birds, rabbits, turtles.

Talk about each one and how we take care of it. What kind of a home does it need to stay in? What does it eat?

(It is also important for the children to understand that there are many animals that are not meant to be kept as domestic pets, but, unfortunately, sometimes people do it. Some exotic birds, hermit crabs, deer and other animals have been harmed by removing them from their natural habitats and taking them into people's homes.)

Hazel was an Only Pet, John Hamberger
Pet Show! Ezra Keats
Polly the Guinea Pig, Margaret Pursell
Nicholas's Favorite Pet, Inger Sandberg
Let's Get Turtles, Millicent Selsam
My Goldfish, Herbert Wong
Two Guppies, a Turtle and Aunt Edna, Lois Wyse
Crictor, Tomi Ungerer
Babar and the Wully-Wully, Laurent and Jean de Brunhoff

Make a parrot puzzle: draw a picture of a parrot on a heavy piece of white paper. Let the children color it as they desire, using lots of bright colors. Glue to a piece of cardboard. When dry, cut out the cardboard into 4 to 10 pieces, depending on the age of the child. Have them practice putting the pieces back together.

Make a pet mobile: draw pictures of a bird, a turtle, a snake, a fish and a rabbit, and have the children color. Attach to a mobile, as shown in Chapter 1.

Visit a pet store and let the children see other kinds of pets that some people own. Or, if you have a neighbor or friend with an unusual pet, make arrangements for your children to visit and watch them care for their pet.

CHAPTER 25
THE WORLD AROUND US

DAY 1	**OUR EARTH**
DAY 2	**THE SUN**
DAY 3	**THE NIGHT SKY**
DAY 4	**RIVERS**
DAY 5	**TREES**
DAY 6	**MOUNTAINS**

Show the children a globe. Talk about the parts that are land and the parts that are sea. (If you don't have a globe, a map of the world will do, if you explain that it is like the world cut open and laid down flat.)

Talk about what lives on the land and what lives in the ocean.

Talk about what parts of the world are hot and what parts of the world are cold.

Show them how part of the world is having night when the other side is having day. This can be shown by placing the globe by a lamp—the other side will be dark.

The Bears' Nature Guide, Stan and Jan Berenstain
Hailstones and Halibut Bones, Mary O'Neill

Take a walk. Talk about the wonderful world we live in. Help the children appreciate the many beauties of nature in their neighborhood or a nearby park. Ask them about the sounds they hear: birds singing, dogs barking, the wind blowing the leaves, etc.

This is also fun to repeat at night. Ask them how things look different than in the daytime. Ask them what sounds they hear now.

DAY 2
THE SUN

Ask the children what is up in the sky that makes it light in the daytime. (the sun)

Tell them that years ago, the people thought the sun went around the earth, but now we know that the earth goes around the sun. They might like to use the word *revolve*.

Talk about the sun as our friend: it heats the world, helps the plants and flowers grow, melts the snow so winter can end, heats many homes.

Talk about how we have to be careful with the sun though: we should not look at it; we can't stay out too long in it or we will get sunburned.

The Day We Saw the Sun Come Up, Alice Goudey
The North Wind and the Sun, Jean De LaFontaine
Follow the Sunset, Herman Schneider
Dawn, Uri Shulevitz
Sun Up, Alvin Tresselt

Inside a black construction-paper frame, glue strips of colored tissue paper to make a rainbow—red, orange, yellow, green, blue, purple. Tape the frame to their window. When the sun shines through the tissue, the colors will appear somewhere on the wall or floor of their room.

To help the children see the movement of the sun through the sky, make a sundial. Cut a 12" circle from cardboard. Place it flat on the ground in some sunny place. Push a sharp dowel or pencil through the center of the cardboard and into the ground, so that it will stand upright. At hourly intervals, mark the sundial where the shadow falls. At the end of a day, you will have a fairly good idea what time it is by looking at the place where the shadow crosses your marks.

Using light-sensitive paper (we get ours at a school supply store), place paper in the sun, covering part of it with another paper design or an object such as a leaf. Soon, the paper will be exposed to the sun and change color, but the covered design will remain. (This can also be done just with dark paper, but it takes several days before the exposed part has faded enough.)

Ask the children what they see when they look up in the sky at night. Ask them where the sun has gone.

Moon: explain to the children that the moon turns around the earth. This is easier for the children to understand if you have a small ball for the moon and a larger one or globe for the earth. Tell them that the moon gets its light from the sun's reflection. Perhaps they have seen what looks like a man in the moon. The "man" is really the shadows of huge craters or holes on the moon.

Stars: children seem to understand best when the stars are explained as small suns far, far away. The stars were used to guide sailors and travelers.

Show the children some pictures of the constellations. Help them imagine the pictures behind the star groups.

Happy Birthday, Moon, Frank Asch
What's in the Dark, Carl Memling
Goodnight Moon, Margaret Brown
Bears in the Night, Stan and Jan Berenstain
What the Moon Saw, Brian Wildsmith
Look at the Moon, May Garelick
Wait til the Moon is Full, Margaret Brown
A Bucketful of Moon, Toby Talbot
Moon Man, Tomi Ungerer
Midnight Moon, Clyde Watson
Goodnight, Eve Rice
The stories or legends behind the constellations

"Twinkle, Twinkle, Little Star"

I see the Moon,
And the Moon sees me.
God bless the Moon,
And God bless me.

"Winken, Blinken and Nod," Eugene Field

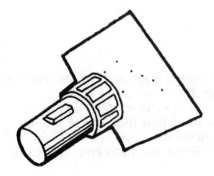

Glue paper stars on black construction paper.

Punch pinholes out of black construction paper in the shape of familiar constellations. Hold against a flashlight in a darkened room. The stars will shine up on the ceiling.

Look at the stars at night.

Show a picture of a river (you can just draw one if you want). Ask the children where the water comes from—the earth (a spring), melting snow, rain.

Make a little "river bed" outside. Run some water from a pitcher or a hose down the trough. Point out that the water took a little dirt with it, too. Thus, the pathway has become deeper. This is called erosion.

Talk about the difference between a brook, a stream and a river—size, how fast the water is moving, how deep it is.

Talk about how rivers help us—watering the land; providing drinks for birds and animals; providing homes for many animals, such as fish, beavers and frogs; making power for the hydroelectric plants or mills; transporting things, such as logs to the lumber mill or food to market.

Where the Brook Begins, Margaret Bartlett
We Live by the River, Lois Lenski
The Boats on the River, Marjorie Flack
Alfie Finds the Other Side of the World,
  Charles Keeping
Tim Mouse Goes Downstream, Judy Brook

Visit a river or stream nearby. Talk about the many things that you see.

Take a boat ride on a river.

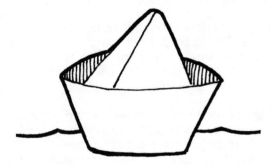

Make a boat as in Chapter 12, Day 5. Watch it sail on the little riverbed you made with the hose.

Make a little raft from Popsicle sticks. Glue 6 Popsicle sticks together on a table. Glue 2 other sticks across the top and bottom for strength. Set it sailing in a river or your bathtub.

Have cutouts of the parts of a tree—trunk, roots, branches, leaves or needles. As you put each up, let the children guess what it is. Help them learn the words after you.

On a walk or with the help of a book, talk about what makes trees different from one another—the height, the bark, the shape and color of the leaves or needles, the seeds, pods or cones for reproduction.

Talk about all the things that trees help us with—lumber to build things with, fuel, shade, erosion prevention, as windbreaks for protection from storms, homes for birds and animals, cleansing of the air.

Talk about the things that we can do to help protect trees—don't tear away the bark, which protects them; be careful not to break branches; don't dig around the trunk and break the roots; watch out for harmful insects that might destroy a tree.

Spooky Old Tree, Stan and Jan Berenstain
A Tree is Nice, Janice Udry
Have You Seen Trees? Joanne Oppenheim
The Dead Tree, Alvin Tresselt
Our Tree, Herbert Wong and Matthew Vessel

Make pinecone animals.

Place a stalk of celery in colored water. The children can watch the color drawn through the stem. Compare that to the way the sap rises through the tree.

Make leaf prints: place flat leaves onto a sheet of heavy paper. Dip a paint brush into tempera paint. Holding it over the paper, gently tap it against a stick and the paint will leave spatters on the paper. When dry, remove the leaf and the outline will remain on the paper.

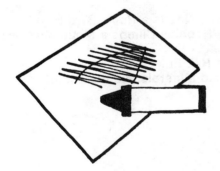

Make tree rubbings, using different parts of the tree—leaves, needles, bark. Place under a piece of paper. Rub over the top with the side of a crayon. The impression will appear on the top sheet of the object underneath.

Have the children pretend that they are giants. Let them eat broccoli, asparagus and celery "trees."

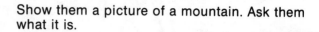

Show them a picture of a mountain. Ask them what it is.

Talk about the many ways that mountains are formed—a stream can cut down earth on either side until eventually mountain walls remain; a volcano can push up the earth from underneath, forming a mountain; sometimes the lava explodes out of the ground, forming a mountain; sometimes the earth folds, or parts of the rock move upward and some move downward. (Again, keep this simple and don't spend a lot of time on it.)

Talk about the animals that live on mountains—goats, coyotes, mountain lions.

Talk about the weather on mountains—colder than at lower altitudes, windy, snowy.

Everybody Needs a Rock, Byrd Baylor
Timothy Robbins Climbs a Mountain, Alvin Tresselt
Bernie's Hill, Erik Blegvad
Rocks and Minerals, Illa Podendorf

"Big Rock Candy Mountain"

"The Bear Went Over the Mountain"

Let the children form mountains out of clay or playdough.

Walk or drive through some mountains.

Make rock animals: find some large pebbles with bumps on them, which look as if they could be something else. Paint the appropriate color and add construction-paper features, if necessary. We have found rocks that look like fish, dogs and a mouse. If you paint them with clear varnish when done, they will stay bright and pretty.

INDEX

Jill Dunford was born and raised in Salt Lake City, Utah. She received her B.A. in education from the University of Utah. She has worked many years as a teacher and teacher-trainer in her church's nursery programs, on both a local and an area level. She has also taught seminars to other mothers on developing their own home nursery programs. Besides raising her seven children, she has been involved in the EDGE (gifted education) program and the summer library reading program; she also serves on the school district orchestra board. The author of magazine articles on children, she currently resides with her family in Dayton, Ohio.

Other Home & Family Books of Interest

Confessions of a Happily Organized Family, by Deniece Schofield. How to work together as a family to restore (or establish!) a comfortable sense of order to your home. You'll find specific techniques for making mornings less hectic, traveling with kids, making chores fun, and more. 246 pages, $7.95, paper

Confessions of an Organized Housewife, by Deniece Schofield. Schofield shares her secrets of household organization and time management, with specific ideas for organizing every aspect of home life—the kitchen, laundry, paperwork, storage areas, and more—to help you take control of your life! 214 pages, $6.95, paper

Is There Life After Housework?, by Don Aslett. America's #1 Cleaning Expert shows you how to save up to 75% of the time you now spend cleaning your home by using the tools and techniques the professionals use. 178 pages, $7.95, paper

Do I Dust or Vacuum First?, by Don Aslett. Here are answers to the 100 most-often-asked housecleaning questions, including how to keep your no-wax floors looking like new and how to clean brick walls. 183 pages, $6.95, paper

Clutter's Last Stand, by Don Aslett. In this "ultimate self-improvement book," Aslett gives you the courage to sift, sort, and toss whatever is detrimental to your housekeeping (and mental!) health—and get rid of clutter once and for all. 276 pages, $8.95, paper

It's Here . . . Somewhere!, by Alice Fulton & Pauline Hatch. Alice and Pauline show you how to get more places out of your spaces with their *room-by-room* approach to getting your home in order. They'll take you step-by-step through every room in your house helping you decide what to keep, how and where to store it, and more. 192 pages, $6.95, paper

Extra Cash for Women, by Susan Gillenwater & Virginia Dennis. Turn your talent, creativity, and energy into extra income with this guide to scores of home-based jobs. Includes tips on how to raise start-up money, advertise your business, and win your family's support. 312 pages, $8.95, paper

Extra Cash for Kids, by Larry Belliston & Kurt Hanks. Kids 8-16 will find more than 100 ways to earn money during summer and spare-time hours, with complete details on how to do the job, equipment needed, and pricing. 185 pages, $6.95, paper

USE THIS COUPON TO ORDER YOUR COPIES TODAY!

_____

YES! Please send me the following books:

_____ (1145) Confessions of a Happily Organized Family, $7.95 ea.

_____ (1143) Confessions of an Organized Housewife, $6.95 ea.

_____ (1455) Is There Life After Housework?, $7.95 ea.

_____ (1214) Do I Dust or Vacuum First?, $6.95 ea.

_____ (1122) Clutter's Last Stand, $8.95 ea.

_____ (1461) It's Here . . . Somewhere!, $6.95 ea.

_____ (1245) Extra Cash for Women, $8.95 ea.

_____ (1246) Extra Cash for Kids, $6.95 ea.

(Please add $2.00 postage & handling for one book, 50¢ for each additional
book. Ohio residents add 5½% sales tax.)   1856

☐ Payment enclosed   ☐ Please charge my: ☐ Visa   ☐ MasterCard

Acct. # _____ Exp. Date _____
Signature _____
Name _____
Address _____
City _____ State _____ Zip _____

Send to: Writer's Digest Books, 9933 Alliance Road, Cincinnati, Ohio 45242

_____